MW01230926

A Soldier's Whisper and Reflections
The Life and Times of SSGT Ralph Lee Butler, Jr.

SSGT Ralph Lee Butler, Jr.

First published by Dog Ear Publishing
4010 W. 86th Street, Ste H
Indianapolis, IN 46268
www.dogearpublishing.net

ISBN: 978-1-4575-2607-7

This book is printed on acid-free paper.

Printed in the United States of America

BROKEN DREAMS

IF TOMORROW
NEVER COMES
TODAY WAS
NEVER LIVED
SO IT MAKES YESTERDAY
NOTHING BUT A DREAM

A DREAM
IS FULL OF HOPE
A DREAM
IS NOTHING BUT FAITH
BUT A BROKEN DREAM
CAN BE A NIGHTMARE
IT'S WHAT LIFE IS MADE OF
BUT HOW CAN YOU LIVE
ON FAITH
AND FAITH ALONE
WITH OUT A DREAM
WE CAN NOT LIVE
WITH OUT A DREAM
WE CAN NOT SEE

IF TOMORROW
NEVER COMES
TODAY WAS
NEVER LIVED
SO IT MAKES YESTERDAY
NOTHING BUT A DREAM

SO BROKEN DREAMS
IS WHAT LIFE IS MADE OF
IT MAKES YOU STRONG
DEEP WITH IN
AND BROKEN DREAMS
ARE NOT SEEN
BUT IT SCARES THE HEART
DEEP WITH IN
FOR TOMORROW
WE HAVE NOT SEEN
FOR TODAY WE WILL NOT LIVE

BECAUSE BROKEN DREAMS
HAVE STRUCK AGAIN

IF TOMORROW
NEVER COMES
TODAY WAS
NEVER LIVED
SO IT MAKES YESTERDAY
NOTHING BUT A DREAM

SO HOW CAN YOU LOVE
SOMEONE
OR SOMETHING
IF YOU DO NOT UNDERSTAND
LOVE ITSELF
THROUGHT HOPE
OR FAITH
NO
NOT AT ALL
IT'S THROUGHT A DREAM
AND A DREAM ALONE
A DREAM WITHIN YOURSELF
SO HOW MANY TIMES
DOES IT TAKE
FOR A DREAM TO FALL
TO REALIZE
THE DREAM
MAY NEVER BE A DREAM

IF TOMORROW
NEVER COMES
TODAY WAS
NEVER LIVED
SO IT MAKES YESTERDAY
NOTHING BUT A DREAM

NO MATTER
HOW OLD WE ARE
OR HOW YOUNG WE ACT
THE DREAMS
OR EVEN BROKEN DREAMS
KEEP US DREAMING ON

FOR TOMORROW IS A DREAM
AND TODAY
IS A BROKEN DREAM
AND YESTERDAY
IS NOTHING BUT HOPE OF A
DREAM

IF TOMORROW
NEVER COMES
TODAY WAS
NEVER LIVED
SO IT MAKES YESTERDAY
NOTHING BUT A DREAM
NOTHING BUT A BROKEN
DREAM

WHO WILL CRY FOR ME

THE WALLS ARE BLACK
THE SKYS ARE DARK

THERE IS NO STARS
THERE IS NO LIGHT

SO WHO WILL CRY FOR ME

YOU SAW ONLY
WHAT YOU WANTED TO SEE

YOU HERD ONLY
WHAT YOU WANTED TO HEAR

AND YOU TOLD ONLY
WHAT YOU WANTED TO TELL

SO WHO WILL CRY FOR ME

SO REMEMBER
IF YOU SEE IT AGAIN

LOOK DEEP
AND SEE IT ALL

LISTEN HARD
AND HEAR IT ALL

THEN TELL SOMONE
AND TELL IT ALL

WITH YOUR VOICE
AND YOUR WORDS

HE MIGHT NOT CRY ALONE

SO REMEMBER
IF YOU SEE IT AGAIN

SSGT RALPH LEE BUTLER, JR.

THE WALLS ARE BLACK
THE SKYS ARE DARK

THERE IS NO STARS
THERE IS NO LIGHT

FOR THE PAIN
HAS NOT BEEN FORGOTTEN

AND THE SCARS
ARE TO DEEP TO MEND

SO PLEASE TELL ME
WHO WILL CRY FOR ME

A MANS HEART
HAS A STORY TO TELL

A MANS HEART
HAS A STORY TO TELL
TO SOMEONE SPECIAL
TO SOMEONE DEAR
OH CAN IT BE
OH CAN IT BE
FOR SOMEONE LIKE ME

AS A BABY
MY HEART WAS PURE
SO PURE AS GOLD
THAT I KNEW NO WRONG
BUT I STILL HUNGERED
FOR THE LOVE OF ANOTHER
AS HIS MOMMA CRYED
HE SAID WITH PRIDE

A MANS HEART
HAS A STORY TO TELL
TO SOMEONE SPECIAL
TO SOMEONE DEAR
OH CAN IT BE
OH CAN IT BE
FOR SOMEONE LIKE ME

AND AS A CHILD
MY HEART GREW COLD
COLDER THAN THE BITTER
SNOWS
SO I HAD SOME HOPE
BUT HOPE FADED AWAY
SO I HAD A DREAM
AND THE DREAM BECAME
NOTHING
BUT A NIGHTMARE

BUT A MANS HEART
HAS A STORY TO TELL
TO SOMEONE SPECIAL

TO SOMEONE DEAR
OH CAN IT BE
OH CAN IT BE
FOR SOMEONE LIKE ME

AND AS A TEEN
I DONE SOME THING
TRYING AND TRYING
TO BE APART OF SOMETHING
I RAN
IN ALL THE WRONG WAYS
I FOUGHT
FOR ALL THE WRONG REASONS
BUT SELF
IS SOON TO BE GONE
AN IMAGE
NO LONGER TO BE

BECAUSE A MANS HEART
HAS A STORY TO TELL
TO SOMEONE SPECIAL
TO SOMEONE DEAR
OH CAN IT BE
OH CAN IT BE
FOR SOMEONE LIKE ME

YEARS MAY COME
AND YEARS MAY GO
OVER AND OVER
I STOOD ALONE
BUT THROUGHT TIME
AND TIME WILL TELL
MY HEART CAN BE
AS PURE AS GOLD

A MANS HEART
HAS A STORY TO TELL
TO SOMEONE SPECIAL
TO SOMEONE DEAR
OH CAN IT BE
OH CAN IT BE
FOR SOMEONE LIKE ME

AND NOW AS A MAN
I CAN SAY WITH PRIDE
I'M TRYING TO GET BACK
WHAT FADED AWAY
HOPE
HOPE THAT WAS LOST
AS A CHILD
AND THE NIGHTMARES
TRYING TO TURN TO DREAMS
DREAMS THAT CAN BE REALITY

BECAUSE A MANS HEART
HAS A STORY TO TELL
TO SOMEONE SPECIAL
TO SOMEONE DEAR
TO SOMEONE LIKE YOU
OH CAN IT BE
OH CAN IT BE
FOR SOMEONE LIKE ME
A MANS HEART
HAS A STORY TO TELL

A TEAR RAN DOWN HIS FACE

A TEAR
RAN DOWN HIS FACE
BECAUSE HE HAD TO GO
TO ANOTHER PLACE
IN AND OUT
OF FOSTERHOMES
ALL ALONG THE WAY
A TEAR
RAN DOWN HIS FACE
BECAUSE HE HAD TO GO
TO ANOTHER PLACE

THE GAMES HE PLAYED
IS WHAT HE HAD LEARNED
FROM HIS MOTHER
ALONG THE WAY

HE KNEW ONE THING
AND HE PLAYED IT
ALL TO WELL

BUT A TEAR
RAN DOWN HIS FACE
BECAUSE HE HAD TO GO
TO ANOTHER PLACE
IN AND OUT
OF FOSTERHOMES
ALL ALONG THE WAY
A TEAR
RAN DOWN HIS FACE
BECAUSE HE HAD TO GO
TO ANOTHER PLACE

WE TRIED TO HELP HIM
ALONG THE WAY
BUT THEIR WAS SOMETHING
ABOUT HIM
THAT NO ONE COULD TOUCH

THE WRITTINGS HE DONE
CAME FROM ABOVE
SO PURE AND TRUE
FOR US TO TRUST

BUT A TEAR
RAN DOWN HIS FACE
BECAUSE HE HAD TO GO
TO ANOTHER PLACE
IN AND OUT
OF FOSTERHOMES
ALL ALONG THE WAY
A TEAR
RAN DOWN HIS FACE
BECAUSE HE HAD TO GO
TO ANOTHER PLACE

AFTER ALL THESE YEARS
I SEE HIM THEIR
AND I WONDER
ABOUT THOSE TEARS

WAS IT A CRY
FOR HELP
OR WAS IT A TEAR
OF SORROW
SOMETHING I WILL NEVER
KNOW
AS A TEAR
RAN DOWN MY FACE
BECAUSE HE HAD TO GO
TO ANOTHER PLACE
IN AND OUT
OF FOSTERHOMES
ALL ALONG THE WAY
A TEAR
RAN DOWN MY FACE
BECAUSE HE WAS NOT
AT OUR PLACE

BUT A TEAR
RAN DOWN HIS FACE

BECAUSE HE HAD TO GO
TO ANOTHER PLACE
IN AND OUT
OF FOSTERHOMES
ALL ALONG THE WAY
A TEAR
RAN DOWN HIS FACE
BECAUSE HE HAD TO GO
TO ANOTHER PLACE

I WISH OUR TEARS
COULD HAVE BEEN
TEARS OF JOY
ALONG THE WAY

BUT NOW OUR TEARS
ARE JOINED AT LAST
BECAUSE HE IS HERE
AT OUR PLACE

BUT THE TEARS
STILL RUN
DOWN OUR FACE
BECAUSE YOU WENT
TO ANOTHER PLACE

EVEN THOUGH I WENT ON
IN MY HEART
AND IN MY MIND
I WAS WITH YOU
EVEN THOUGH
I WAS GONE
YOU WHERE STILL
MOM AND DAD
TO ME

I FEEL
I WILL ALWAYS BE
YOUR SON
LITTLE HARV
THAT YOU WANTED
TO ADOPT

SO THANKS
AND THANKS AGAIN
FOR BEING
MOM AND DAD
TO ME

I WILL ALWAYS
BE SORRY
FOR WHAT I HAD DONE
TO MY BROTHERS
AND YOU

SO A TEAR
WILL ALWAYS RUN
DOWN MY FACE
WHEN I THINK
ABOUT YOUR PLACE

SSGT RALPH LEE BUTLER, JR.

JUST LISTEN
<u>TO ME FOR ONCE</u>

PLEASE REMEMBER
KEEP YOUR HANDS
TO YOURSELF
THERE HAS BEEN ENOUGH
HITTING AND SCREAMING
SO PLEASE REMEMBER
KEEP YOUR VOICE DOWN
FOR THE PAIN
HAS NOT BEEN FORGOTTEN
AND THE SCARS
ARE TO DEEP TO MEND
SO PLEASE REMEMBER
KEEP YOUR HANDS
TO YOURSELF
THERE HAS BEEN ENOUGH
HITTING AND SCREAMING
SO PLEASE REMEMBER
KEEP YOUR VOICE DOWN

IT ALL STARTED
WHEN I WAS YOUNG
IN A WORLD
THAT I THOUHGT WAS FUN
I DID NOT ASK
TO BE HERE
YOU'RE THE ONE
WHO DID THAT FOR ME
AND REMEMBER WHEN YOU
LEFT ME WITH SOME FRIENDS
WEEKS ON END

PLEASE REMEMBER
KEEP YOUR HANDS
TO YOURSELF
THERE HAS BEEN ENOUGH
HITTING AND SCREAMING
SO PLEASE REMEMBER
KEEP YOUR VOICE DOWN
FOR THE PAIN

HAS NOT BEEN FORGOTTEN
AND THE SCARS
ARE TO DEEP TO MEND
SO PLEASE REMEMBER
KEEP YOUR HANDS
TO YOURSELF
THERE HAS BEEN ENOUGH
HITTING AND SCREAMING
SO PLEASE REMEMBER
KEEP YOUR VOICE DOWN

WHEN TIME WENT ON
SO DID YOU
YOU TURNED YOUR BACK
AND YOU WENT ON
WITH YOUR LIFE
MAKING OTHERS TO DECIDE
WHAT TO DO
WITH ME
AND YOU'RE THE ONE
THAT SAID
YOU'RE AN UNFIT MOTHER
AND NO LONGER WANTS
TO PROVIDE CARE
FOR YOUR CHILD

PLEASE REMEMBER
KEEP YOUR HANDS
TO YOURSELF
THERE HAS BEEN ENOUGH
HITTING AND SCREAMING
SO PLEASE REMEMBER
KEEP YOUR VOICE DOWN
FOR THE PAIN
HAS NOT BEEN FORGOTTEN
AND THE SCARS
ARE TO DEEP TO MEND
SO PLEASE REMEMBER
KEEP YOUR HANDS
TO YOURSELF
THERE HAS BEEN ENOUGH
HITTING AND SCREAMING

SO PLEASE REMEMBER
KEEP YOUR VOICE DOWN

YOU SIGNED IT IN INK
JUST AS IF IT WAS BLOOD
BECAUSE THEY CAN SEE
THE SCARS YOU LEFT IN ME
YOU SAID
IT WAS FOR ME
BUT WHEN YOU LOOK BACK
YOU WILL SEE
YOU DID IT FOR YOU
AND YOUR GREED

PLEASE REMEMBER
KEEP YOUR HANDS
TO YOURSELF
THERE HAS BEEN ENOUGH
HITTING AND SCREAMING
SO PLEASE REMEMBER
KEEP YOUR VOICE DOWN
FOR THE PAIN
HAS NOT BEEN FORGOTTEN
AND THE SCARS
ARE TO DEEP TO MEND
SO PLEASE REMEMBER
KEEP YOUR HANDS
TO YOURSELF
THERE HAS BEEN ENOUGH
HITTING AND SCREAMING
SO PLEASE REMEMBER
KEEP YOUR VOICE DOWN

I HAD A HOME
AND A FAMILY
THAT TRIED TO GIVE ME
WHAT I HAD LONGED FOR
BUT WHAT DID YOU SAY
ARE YOU GOING
TO LEAVE YOUR MOMMY
THAT YOU STILL WANT ME
AND THAT YOU STILL LOVE ME

THAT YOU WERE NOT GOING
TO LET THEM ADOPT ME
SORRY TO SAY
THAT WAS YOUR GREED
ABOUT YOU
AND YOU ALONE

PLEASE REMEMBER
KEEP YOUR HANDS
TO YOURSELF
THERE HAS BEEN ENOUGH
HITTING AND SCREAMING
SO PLEASE REMEMBER
KEEP YOUR VOICE DOWN
FOR THE PAIN
HAS NOT BEEN FORGOTTEN
AND THE SCARS
ARE TO DEEP TO MEND
SO PLEASE REMEMBER
KEEP YOUR HANDS
TO YOURSELF
THERE HAS BEEN ENOUGH
HITTING AND SCREAMING
SO PLEASE REMEMBER
KEEP YOUR VOICE DOWN

YOU THINK ABOUT YOURSELF
AND THE COST
IS AT YOUR CHILDS EXPENSE
YOU NEVER CARED ENOUGH
ABOUT ME
YOU JUST PUSHED ME AWAY
AND CLOSED THE DOOR
SO YOU NEVER SAW
THE PAIN OR THE TEARS
BECAUSE YOU ALWAYS BLAMED
SOMEONE ELSE
FOR WHAT YOU HAD DONE

PLEASE REMEMBER
KEEP YOUR HANDS
TO YOURSELF

SSGT RALPH LEE BUTLER, JR.

THERE HAS BEEN ENOUGH
HITTING AND SCREAMING
SO PLEASE REMEMBER
KEEP YOUR VOICE DOWN
FOR THE PAIN
HAS NOT BEEN FORGOTTEN
AND THE SCARS
ARE TO DEEP TO MEND
SO PLEASE REMEMBER
KEEP YOUR HANDS
TO YOURSELF
THERE HAS BEEN ENOUGH
HITTING AND SCREAMING
SO PLEASE REMEMBER
KEEP YOUR VOICE DOWN

BUT THE LAST TIME
YOU RAISED THAT HAND
AND YOUR VOICE
IT WAS LIKE IT WAS
BACK THEN
SO I TURNED
AND I GAVE IT BACK
THE WAY YOU
DELT IT BACK THEN
YOU AGAIN
TOLD ME TO LEAVE
AND DON'T COME BACK
AND THEN YOU WANTED
AN ANSWER
AND THIS IS WHAT I SAID

PLEASE REMEMBER
KEEP YOUR HANDS
TO YOURSELF
THERE HAS BEEN ENOUGH
HITTING AND SCREAMING
SO PLEASE REMEMBER
KEEP YOUR VOICE DOWN
FOR THE PAIN
HAS NOT BEEN FORGOTTEN
AND THE SCARS
ARE TO DEEP TO MEND

SO PLEASE REMEMBER
KEEP YOUR HANDS
TO YOURSELF
THERE HAS BEEN ENOUGH
HITTING AND SCREAMING
SO PLEASE REMEMBER
KEEP YOUR VOICE DOWN

I TOLD YOU ONCE
AND I'LL TELL YOU AGAIN
YOU DID IT TO ME
BACK THEN
BUT YOU WILL NOT
DO IT AGAIN
FOR I AM NOT
THE SAME LITTLE KID
THAT YOU KNEW
BACK THEN
FOR I AM
A SPECIAL PERSON
BECAUSE I MADE IT
TO THE END
SO PLEASE REMEMBER
IF YOU SEE ME AGAIN
REMEMBER TO
KEEP YOUR HANDS
TO YOURSELF
THERE HAS BEEN ENOUGH
HITTING AND SCREAMING
SO PLEASE REMEMBER
KEEP YOUR VOICE DOWN
FOR THE PAIN
HAS NOT BEEN FORGOTTEN
AND THE SCARS
ARE TO DEEP TO MEND
SO PLEASE REMEMBER
KEEP YOUR HANDS
TO YOURSELF
THERE HAS BEEN ENOUGH
HITTING AND SCREAMING
SO PLEASE REMEMBER
KEEP YOUR VOICE DOWN

A MAN DON'T YOU SEE

I'M LIKE A STEAM
ON A TRIP
FLOWING
SO SOFT
AND FREE
WITH THE MIST
OF RAIN
I'LL SOON GROW
INTO A RIVER
RUNNING SO FREE
WITH SEVERAL
STANDING PIONTS
ALONG THE WAY
BUT
IN HEAVEY RAINS
I'LL BECOME
INRAGED
PUSHING
AND SHUVING
EVERTHING
OUT OF MY WAY
BUT I'LL
SOON CALM DOWN
WHEN
THE RAINS QUITE
AND
I'LL FIND MYSELF
AT THE WATERS FRONT
IN A LAND
OF WATER
A PLACE
CALLED AN OCEAN
THAT ALL CAN SEE
AND SAY
HE WAS A STREAM
IN THE MIST
OF RAIN
RUNNING
SO WILD
AND FREE

AND
LOOK AT HIM NOW
HE HAS BECOME
APART OF THE OCEAN
A MAN
DON'T YOU SEE

SSGT RALPH LEE BUTLER, JR.

TO SEEK

FROM PEAK TO PEAK
TO ROCK TO ROCK

FROM MEADOW TO MEADOW
TO SEA TO SEA

WHAT SHALL I SEEK
FROM ALL OF THESE

TO SEEK
YOU MUST GO ON A TRIP
WHERE NO MAN IS FOUND
FOR MILES AROUND

WHERE THE DEER CAN ROAM
AND THE SQUIRRELS CAN PLAY

WHERE THE EAGLES FLY
AND THE RIVERS RUN FREE

WHERE THE SUN SHINES
AND THE MOON IS BRIGHT

WHERE THE STARS GLOW
AND YOU CAN SEE AT NIGHT

AND IT ALL BRINGS OUT
THE WILD LIFE

A PLACE LIKE THIS
IS NOT A DREAM

IT'S A PLACE
OF PEACE AND MIND

FROM PEAK TO PEAK
TO ROCK TO ROCK

FROM MEADOW TO MEADOW
TO SEA TO SEA

THAT IS WHAT I SEEK
IN ALL OF THESE

FREEDOM IS HERE

THIS GREAT NATION
HAS A STORY
LIKE NO OTHER

IT ALL STARTS
WITH OUR FLAG

THESE COLORS MIGHT FADE
BUT THEY WILL NOT RUN

THE COLORS ARE RED
TO SHOW THE WORLD
WHAT WE HAVE SHED

THE COLORS ARE WHITE
TO SHOW THE WORLD
THAT WE WILL FIGHT

AND THE COLORS ARE BLUE
TO SHOW THE WORLD
THAT WE ARE TRUE

IT WAS SEPTEMBER 11
THAT TOOK A TOLL

BUT IF WE LOOK CLOSE
IT CAME TO US
WITH A CALL OF 911

THAT WHAT DID FADE
CAME OUT STRONG
ALL ACROSS OUR LAND

ON POLLS
ON WALLS
ON BUILDINGS
AND EVEN ON OUR CARS

OUR GREAT NATION
CAME ALIVE

LIKE NO OTHER

THIS IS A TIME
FOR FREEDOM TO STAND OUT

FROM BROTHER TO BROTHER
TO SISTER TO SISTER
FROM STATE TO STATE
THAT'S WHAT MAKES
THE U.S.A.

FREEDOM
FREEDOM WE YELL
FREEDOM HAS BEEN CALLED
OUT
AND OUR FLAG
IS STILL HERE

ITS GOING TO BE
PEOPLE FIGHTING
FIGHTING FOR LIBERTY
FIGHTING FOR FREEDOM

BUT THERE ARE MANY HERO'S
IN THIS GREAT NATION

THEY RANGE
FROM WORLD WAR I
TO WORLD WAR II
THE KOREAN WAR
TO VIETNAM
FROM DESERT STORM
TO OPERATION ENDURING
FREEDOM

BUT STILL
THEIR WILL BE A PRICE
FOR OUR FREEDOM

IT WILL BE
PEOPLE DIEING
DIEING FOR LIBERTY

SSGT RALPH LEE BUTLER, JR.

DIEING FOR FREEDOM

SO
WHEN THE FIRE QUITS
AND THE SMOKE CLEARS
YOU WILL SEE
OUR FLAG IS STILL HERE

AND
THIS IS THE PRICE
WE WILL PAY
WITH BLOOD
SWEAT
AND TEARS

BUT FREEDOM IS HERE

FREEDOM
IS HERE

WAVING BACK

I LIKE TO STAND TALL
AND SHOW THE WORLD
WHO I AM

SOME OF YOU
HAVE FOUGHT FOR ME

WHILE OTHERS
HAVE TORN ME DOWN

BUT I WILL
ALWAYS SURVIVE

BECAUSE I DO
HAVE AN ATTITUDE

AND I SHOW
MY COLORS WELL

I HAVE SEVERAL NAMES
KNOWN THREW THIS LAND

LIKE OLD GLORY
STAR SPANGLED BANNER
THAT FLAG
THE OLD RED WHITE AND
BLUE

BUT I SAY UNTO YOU
I'M YOUR FLAG

AND NOW
WE'LL HAVE THIS TALK
JUST YOU AND ME

DO YOU REMEMBER WHEN
I LEAD THE WAY
TO GAMES
PARADES
AND OTHER THINGS

WHEN YOUR DADDY
SAW ME COMING
AND HE REMOVED HIS HAT

THEN HE TOOK HIS HAND
AND COVERED HIS CHEST

DO YOU REMEMBER THAT

HE DOES
AND SO DOES HIS DADDIES
DAD

WELL
I'M STILL THE SAME OLD FLAG

BUT I HAVE ADDED
SOME STRIPES
AND STARS
SINCE THEN

AND A LOT OF PEOPLE
HAVE DIED FOR ME

BUT I DON'T FEEL AS STRONG
AS I USE TO FEEL

BECAUSE
SOME OF YOU SEE ME
AND YOU DON'T DO A THING

YAH
I MIGHT GET A GLANCE

BUT THEN YOU LOOK
THE OTHER WAY

AND WHEN THE KIDS
ARE RUNNING AROUND
SHOUTING OUT LOUD

THEY JUST DON'T KNOW
WHO I AM
OR
WHAT I STAND FOR

DO YOU REMEMBER
WHEN YOUR DADDY
SAW ME STANDING TALL

AND
HIS EYES
BEGAN TO GLOW

HE TOOK OFF HIS HAT
AND
SO DID YOU

BUT YOU LOOKED AROUND
AND
NO ONE ELSE
HAD THEIRS OFF

SO YOU QUICKLY
PUT YOURS BACK ON

AND AT THE GAME
THEY PLAYED MY SONG

I WAS WAVING AT YOU
TRYING TO GET YOU
TO SING ALONG

BUT I THINK YOU FORGOT
WHAT TO SAY
OR WHAT TO DO

YAH
YOU STOOD UP ALL RIGHT

WITH A DIFFERENT
KIND OF STANCE

THEN YOU STARTED TAKING
AMONG YOURSELVES
ABOUT ODDS AND ENDS
THIS AND THAT'S

SURE I WAS HURT
AND IT HURT REAL BAD
JUST TO SEE
WHAT THIS GENERATION
HAS TO BRING

ARE YOU ASHAMED OF ME
OR HAVE YOU
JUST FORGOTTEN ME

IF SO
REMEMBER THE MEN
AND WOMEN
LIKE YOUR DAD

WHO GAVE THEIR LIVES
FOR THIS LAND

JUST TO KEEP IT FREE

DO YOU REMEMBER WHEN
HE SALUTED ME
HE WAS SALUTING
THEM TOO

AND WHEN HE HONORED ME
HE WAS HONORING
THEM TOO

SO WHEN I'M SINGING
OR JUST WAVING
I'M LOOKING AT YOU

SO STAND UP STRAIGHT
TAKE OFF THAT HAT
PUT YOUR RIGHT HAND
OVER YOUR HEART

BECAUSE
WE ARE SALUTING YOU
BY WAVING BACK

AN AMERICAN HERO

I DID WHAT I WAS I TOLD
AND
I DID IT WITH PRIDE
I DIDN'T ASK QUESTION
I DIDN'T ASK WHY
BECAUSE
I'M AN AMERICAN SOLDIER

I'M NOT PROUD
OF SOME OF THE THINGS
THAT I HAD DONE
OR
EVEN SOME OF THE THINGS
THAT ARE TO COME
BUT I AM
AN AMERICAN SOLDIER

AND AT THIS PRICE
WE HAVE LOST SOME FRIENDS
AND WE HAVE LOST SOME
LIVES
BUT I'M STILL
AN AMERICAN SOLDIER

I WAS ONE OF THE CHOSEN
ONES
BECAUSE
I AM WHAT I AM
BUT THEY SAY
I'M AN AMERICAN HERO
BECAUSE
I'M STILL ALIVE

THEY SAY
IT IS A GOOD DAY TO DIE
BUT TODAY
IS NOT MY DAY
BECAUSE
I'M AN AMERICAN SOLDIER
AND FOR THIS

YOU CALL ME
AN AMERICAN HERO TODAY

BUT WHEN I LOOK BACK
I CAN SAY WITH PRIDE
I'M AN AMERICAN SOLDIER

BUT THOSE
THAT HAVE LOST THEIR LIVES
AND THOSE
THAT WHERE LEFT BEHIND
THEY ARE THE TRUE
AMERICAN HERO'S
AND I WILL ALWAYS BE
AN AMERICAN SOLDIER

SSGT RALPH LEE BUTLER, JR.

A NOTE LONG OVER DUE

I JUST WANTED
TO LET YOU KNOW
HOW LUCKY
OF A GUYI AM

TO HAVE FOUND
SOMEONE LIKE YOU

THAT'S SO LOVING
AND CARING

THAT I HOPE
I'LL NEVER
LET YOU DOWN

BUT IF I FALL
LEND ME A HAND

AND IF I DRIFT
SET SAIL WITH ME

AND IF I FLY
SPREAD YOUR WINGS
SO WE'LL BE
ON TOP OF THINGS TOGETHER

I'M ONE LUCKY GUY
TO HAVE
SOMEONE LIKE YOU

HOW LUCKY CAN I BE

HOW LUCKY CAN I BE
TO HAVE
TO HOLD
AND TO LOVE
SOMEONE LIKE YOU

HOW LUCKY CAN I BE
TO BE WITH
TO SHARE WITH
AND TO GROW WITH
SOMEONE LIKE YOU

HOW LUCKY CAN I BE
TO CARE FOR
TO DO FOR
AND TO LIVE FOR
SOMEONE LIKE YOU

OH
HOW LUCKY CAN I BE

THE THINGS YOU DO

WHEN I'M DOWN
YOU BRING ME UP

WHEN I'M WEAK
YOU MAKE ME STRONG

WHEN I'M SAD
YOU MAKE ME HAPPY

WHEN I CRY
YOU HOLD ME TIGHT

BUT MOST OF ALL
WHEN I HOLD YOUR HAND
OR LOOK INTO YOUR EYES
I CAN FEEL
AND I CAN SEE
THE LOVE
YOU HAVE FOR ME

ALL I CAN DO
IS HOPE
AND PRAY
THAT I DO
THE SAME FOR YOU
THAT YOU DO FOR ME

A TREE OF LOVE

SOME PEOPLE NEVER SEE
HOW FAR
LOVE CAN GROW

SOME PEOPLE NEVER SEE
HOW HIGH
LOVE CAN CLIMB

SOME PEOPLE NEVER SEE
HOW FAST
LOVE CAN MOVE

FROM THE RIVERS
TO THE OCEANS

FROM THE MEADOWS
TO THE VALLEYS

FROM THE DESERTS
TO THE PLAINS

MY LOVE FOR YOU
GROWS IN ALL OF THESE

SO IF YOU LOOK DEEP
YOU WILL SEE

THE MINES
CAN NOT MINE
OUR LOVE AWAY

THE WINDS
CAN NOT BLOW
OUR LOVE AWAY

THE WATERS
CAN NOT WASH
OUR LOVE AWAY

SSGT RALPH LEE BUTLER, JR.

SO MY LOVE FOR YOU
GOES DEEPER
THAN THE ROOTS

IT IS STRONGER
THAN THE BRANCHES

IT IS HIGHER
THAN THE CREST

BECAUSE WE
PLANTED OUR LOVE
ON SOLID GROUND

WITH LOVE
AND TENDER CARE

HAPPY ANNIVERSARY
WITH
A TREE OF LOVE

I DIDN'T GET TO SAY GOODBYE

I WISH I WAS THERE
TO SAY GOODBYE
BUT I WAS SOMEWHERE
OUT THERE
ON THE ROAD
MANY MILES AWAY
BUT IN MY HEART
I WAS THERE
BUT
I DIDN'T GET TO SY GOODBYE

I WAS THERE
WHEN IT ALL STARTED
I SAW THE PAIN
AND THE TEARS
I SAW YOU SMILE
AND
TRY TO TALK
SO I HELD YOUR HAND
AND
YOU SMILED AGAIN
I TOLD YOU TO GET WELL
SO I CAN GET SOME
HOME MADE BREAD
AND
YOU LAUGHED A LITTLE
WITH A WONDERFUL SMILE

WELL
IT WAS TIME TO GO
SO I WENT ON
NEVER THE LESS
I NEVER SAID GOODBYE

BUT
NOW I SEE YOU THERE
AND YOU'RE NOT IN PAIN
YOU STILL HAVE THAT GLOW
AND

YOU'RE IN A BETTER PLACE
SO NOW
I CAN SAY GOODBYE
BECAUSE
I WILL SEE YOU AGAIN
IN ANOTHER PLACE
AND TIME
SO THIS IS NOT GOODBYE

YOUR DADDY'S SIDE

TO LOVE ON EARTH
IS ONLY SHORT LIVED
BUT OUR LOVE IN HEAVEN
WILL ALWAYS LIVE
SO MY LOVE FOR YOU
WILL ALWAYS SHOW
FROM YOUR MOTHER
ON TO YOU
WITH THE DAUGHTERS OF
MINE
YOUR MOTHER
WILL ALWAYS SHINE THROUGH
I SEE IN YOU
THE LOVE WE HAD
EVEN THOUGH
SHE IS GONE
SHE STILL LIVES
IN ALL OF YOU
SO REMEMBER
THE LOVE WE HAVE
IT ALL STARTED
WITH YOUR MOTHER

"LOVE DAD"

A LOVING TRIBUTE

We Know Now
You're At Peace
Because You Have Gone
To Another Place
A Place
You Have Longed For
For A Long, Long Time
You Picked The Time
You Picked The Place
And Now
You're On Your Way
To Be Reunited
With Your Long Lost Love
So Now
We Can Lay You To Rest
With A Yellow Rose
That You Can Take To Mom
We Now
That You Wanted To Take It
To Her In Person
And It's Like You Said
To Love On Earth
Is Only Short Lived
But Our Love In Heaven
Will Always Live

"Your Loving Children"

YOUR SHOES

ANOTHER HERO IS LAID TO
REST
I SALUTE YOU WITH HONORS
AND I'LL TRY TO FIT YOUR
SHOES

YOU'RE THE FATHER
THAT YOUR DAUGHTERS
LOOKED UP TO

YOU'RE THE GRANDFATHER
THAT YOUR GRANDKIDS
LOVED TO BE WITH

YOU'RE THE ONE
THAT HELD YOUR BIBLE
AND HAD US PRAY HAND IN
HAND

YOU ASKED FOR VERY LITTLE
AND WE ALL TRIED TO GIVE
YOU MORE
BECAUSE YOU DESERVED A LOT
MORE

SO YOUR SHOES
WILL BE HARD TO FILL
BECAUSE THEY ARE FILLED
WITH YOU

SO I SALUTE YOU
AS I STAND IN YOUR SHOES
AND IT'S AN HONOR
AS I TRY TO WALK IN THESE
SHOES

QUESTIONS AND ANSWERS

IN THIS WORLD
THERE ARE MANY
QUESTIONS
AND MANY
ANSWERS

BUT

IN THIS LIFE
THERE ARE MANY
QUESTIONS
WITH NO
ANSWERS

AND

IN THIS LIFE
THERE ARE MANY
ANSWERS
WITH NO
QUESTIONS

BUT

IN THIS WORLD
THERE ARE MANY
QUESTIONS
AND MANY
ANSWERS

MY FAMILY DREAM

I TOOK A TRIP
NOT KNOWING
WHAT I WOULD SEE
OR WHAT I WOULD FIND

MANY YEARS
HAVE GONE BY
BUT MY DREAM
WAS STILL ALIVE

I TOOK A TRIP
NOT KNOWING
WHAT I WOULD SEE
OR WHAT I WOULD FIND

FROM CALIFORNIA
TO WYOMING
AND THEN TO OKLAHOMA
A SOONER
IS WHAT I'LL BE

I TOOK A TRIP
NOT KNOWING
WHAT I WOULD SEE
OR WHAT I WOULD FIND

FROM A CHILD
TO A MAN
IS WHAT
I'LL LEARN TO BE

I TOOK A TRIP
NOT KNOWING
WHAT I WOULD SEE
OR WHAT I WOULD FIND

WITH MANY TEARS
THAT WAS LEFT BEHIND
AND A LOT OF PAIN
I DID NOT SEE

I TOOK A TRIP
NOT KNOWING
WHAT I WOULD SEE
OR WHAT I WOULD FIND

THEY SAY CALIFORNIA
IS A PLACE TO BE
WITH GOLD
AND OPPORTUNITY

I TOOK A TRIP
NOT KNOWING
WHAT I WOULD SEE
OR WHAT I WOULD FIND

BUT I FOUND MIND
THE SECOND TIME AROUND
RIGHT HERE WITH YOU
FOR ALL TO SEE

I TOOK A TRIP
NOT KNOWING
WHAT I WOULD SEE
OR WHAT I WOULD FIND

BUT WHEN I CAME BACK
ALL MY TEARS
TURNED TO GOLD
AND THE PAIN
HAS TURNED TO JOY

I TOOK A TRIP
NOT KNOWING
WHAT I WOULD SEE
OR WHAT I WOULD FIND

ON THIS TRIP
I FOUND THE LOVE
SO KIND AND FREE
THAT I WOULD LIKE
TO SAY
I LOVE YOU ALL

MORE AND MORE
EACH AND EVERY DAY

I TOOK A TRIP
NOT KNOWING
WHAT I WOULD SEE
OR WHAT I WOULD FIND

BUT WHAT I SEE
AND WHAT I FOUND
IS MY FAMILY
SO THIS TRIP
WAS MY NEED

I TOOK A TRIP
NOT KNOWING
WHAT I WOULD SEE
OR WHAT I WOULD FIND

THREE WEEKS AT A TIME

AS THE DAY TIME ENDS
AND
THE NIGHT TIME FALLS

A SINGLE BIG RIG
ROLLS DOWN
ON A LONG
DARK ROAD

DODGING THE SCALES
BECAUSE IM OVER WEIGHT

SNEAKING DOWN
THE BACK ROADS
INTO THE NEXT STATE

IM MASHING MY MOTOR
HAULING THIS FREIGHT
DOING MY BEST
TRYING NOT TO BE LATE

AS HEADLIGHTS APPROACH
IN THE DARK
OF THE NIGHT
I BACK IT DOWN
TO FIND ANOTHER
BIG RIG
THAT PASSES IN THE NIGHT

AS HE ROLLS ON
AND OUT OF SIGHT

I KEY UP MY MIC
AND HAULER OUT

HEY EAST BOUND
I HAVE NOT SEEN NOTHING
SO HAMMER ON DOWN
AND
HAVE A GOOD NIGHT

I HEAR HIM KEY UP
AND
TELLS ME THE SAME
THAT I LOOK GOOD
TO THE STATE LINE

THE CB GOES QUIET
AND THERES SILENCE AGAIN

SO I REV UP MY MOTOR
AND WORK THROUGH THE
GEARS

AS THE SUN COMES UP
AND
BRIGHTENS THE DAY

I GOT 100 MORE MILES
TO THE END OF MY DAY

AS I ARRIVE
AND
BACK INTO THE DOCK

HERE COMES THE LUMPERS
THAT WANTS TO
UNLOAD MY TRUCK

SO I PICK ONE OUT
AND
PAY HIM A CHECK

AFTER AN HOUR
IM READY TO ROLL

ONLY 100 MILES
TO MY NEXT LOAD

WELL
WHAT DO YOU KNOW
ITS MY LUCKY DAY

SSGT RALPH LEE BUTLER, JR.

ITS PRELOADED

SO I GET TO
DROP AND HOOK

IM SHORT ON MY HOURS

BUT I STILL GOT TO GO
BECAUSE
IT'S A HOT LOAD

DODGEING MORE SCALES
ON THESE OLD COUNTRY
ROADS

IM MASHING MY MOTOR
AND
HAULING MY LOAD

AS THE NIGHT ROLLS IN
ON THIS LONG STRECH
OF ROAD

SIX MORE HOURS
TO GET THROUGH THE NIGHT

I GET MY SECOND WIND
AT THE FIRST BREAK OF LIGHT

WITH A LONG TRIP
BEHIND ME
AND A SHORT WAY TO GO

I TURN DOWN THE CB
AND PICK UP THE PHONE

TO TELL MY WIFE
ILL BE ROLLING
ON BY

BEFORE SHE HANGS UP
SHE TELLS ME

SHELL SEE ME OUT THERE
ON THE ROAD

AS I PULL INTO THE TRUCK
STOP
TO GET SOME FUEL

LONG AND BEHOLD
THERE SHE IS
WITH DINNER IN HAND

I TAKE MY BREAK
AND SPEND SOME TIME
WITH THIS LADY OF MINE

MY LOG BOOKS CAUGHT UP
AND
ITS TIME TO ROLL

BUT THIS LOAD
JUST GOT RELAYED
AND
I GET TO GO HOME

I SAY TO MY SELF
AS I TURN BACK AROUND

THIS TRIP IS OVER
AND
I GET TO GO HOME

3 DAYS AT HOME
TO REST MY BODY
AND SOUL

MY PIECE OF MIND
IS AT REST
WHEN IM AT HOME

MY 3 DAYS ARE GONE
MY HOME TIME IS UP

WITH A FRESH 70 TO ROLL
ILL START UP MY TRUCK

MY WIFE
LOST IN TEARS
AS I FIRE IT UP

I PULL BACK OUT
ON THIS LONELY ROAD
AS IM WINDING IT UP

I PRAY ONCE MORE
TO THE MAN UP STAIRS

THIS JOB IS NOT EASY
BUT ILL TAKE IT IN STRIDE
SO BUCKEL ME IN
FOR ANOTHER LONG RIDE
KEEP ME SAFE
AND ALIVE
MAKE THESE 3 WEEKS
FLY ON BY

EASE OFF THE GAS

YOU GOT FAST TRUCKS
YOU GOT SLOW TRUCKS
YOU GOT TRUCKS
THAT ARE SOMEWHERE
IN BEWTEEN

SO MASH ON YOUR MOTOR
AND MASH ON YOUR GAS
AT A HIGH RATE
OF FUEL CONSUMPTION
SO YOU WILL NOT BE PASSED

YOU GOT COMPANY RULES
YOU GOT HIGHWAY LAWS
AND LETS NOT FORGET
ABOUT THE DOT

SO EASE OFF THE MOTOR
EASE OFF THE GAS
AND TURN THAT BONUS
INTO SOME CASH

ITS 6.5
OR ANYTHING ABOVE
ITS 65 AND UNDER
THAT WILL HELP YOU
MAKE THAT EXTRA BUCK

SO KEEP IT
BETWEEN THE LINES
AND BIDE YOUR TIME
THE OUT OF ROUTE MILES
WILL DO THE SAME
AND LOOK OUT
FOR THAT LONG IDLE TIME

SO EASE OF THE MOTOR
EASE OFF THE GAS
AND TURN THAT BONUS
INTO SOME CASH

SSGT RALPH LEE BUTLER, JR.

AT THE END
OF THE MONTH
AT THE END
OF THE YEAR
YOU CAN MAKE
THEIR CHRISTMAS
A BETTER CHEER

SO EASE OFF THE MOTOR
AND EASE OFF THE GAS
SO YOU CAN TURN BONUS
INTO SOME CASH

AFTER TWENTY SOME YEARS
THIS IS YOU YEAR

TWENTY SOME YEARS
IS A PRETTY LONG TIME

KIDS HAVE COME
AND KIDS HAVE GONE
ALL IN THIS TIME

YOU WATCHED THEM GROW
AND MARRY OFF
HAVING KIDS OF THEIR OWN

YOU HAVE BEEN A MOTHER
TO SOME
AND A TRUE FRIEND
TO OTHERS
AND TO SOME OF US
EVEN A SISTER

TWENTY SOME YEARS
IS A PRETTY LONG TIME

YOU DROVE THE KIDS
TO AND FROM SCHOOL
AND EVEN SOME
OF THEIR KIDS
THROUGH THESE YEARS

YOU HAVE SEEN
A LOT OF STAFF
COME AND GO
SOME YOU WISH
HAD NEVER GONE

BUT THEY WILL REMEMBER
THE THINGS YOU DID
IN THESE YEARS

YOU HAVE WORKED
MANY HOURS

ALL ON YOUR OWN
USING YOUR CAR
FOR ODDS AND ENDS
EVEN WORKING WEEKENDS

TWENTY SOME YEARS
IS A PRETTY LONG TIME

YOU WANTED THINGS
TO BE JUST RIGHT
SO YOU HELPED OTHERS
ALONG THE WAY

I'VE SEEN YOU PUT THINGS
ASIDE
TO HELP THE STAFF
EVEN WHEN YOU WERE AT
HOME
THE PHONE WOULD RING
COMMUNITY AND STAFF
CALLING FOR YOU
IT WAS AS IF
WORK WOULD NEVER END

BUT TWENTY SOME YEARS
IS A PRETTY LONG TIME

YOU HAVE SEEN THE JOY
AND YOU HAVE SEEN THE
TEARS
THROUGH THESE YEARS
BUT THIS IS YOUR YEAR

WE WILL MISS YOU
MORE THAN WHAT WORDS
CAN SAY
BECAUSE YOU HAVE MADE AN
IMPRESSION
ALONG THE WAY

THE HARD WORK
AND DEDICATION

THAT YOU WILL LEAVE BEHIND
IT'S LIKE A MODEL
AND A TROPHY
THAT WILL BE HARD
TO REPLACE

TWENTY SOME YEARS
IS A PRETTY LONG TIME

I KNOW AT ONE TIME
OR ANOTHER
WE HAVE LAUGHED TOGETHER
AND WE HAVE CRIED
TOGETHER
WE HAVE EVEN HELD ONE
ANOTHER
THROUGH THESE YEARS

WE HAVE WORKED
MANY HOURS TOGETHER
AT THE GAMES
AND OTHER THINGS

YOU HAVE SEEN
MORE THAN YOUR SHARE
IN THESE TWENTY SOME YEARS
SO PLEASE REMEMBER
THIS IS YOUR YEAR

SO TWENTY SOME YEARS
IS A PRETTY LONG TIME

YOU WILL BE MISSED
A LOT MORE THAN YOU KNOW
BUT THE THINGS YOU DID
WILL STILL CARRY ON

THIS IS YOUR TIME
FOR US TO SAY
THANKS AGAIN
FOR HANGIN' IN
BECAUSE WE MAY NOT HAVE

MADE IT
THROUGH THESE YEARS
WITHOUT YOUR SUPPORT
AND YOUR FRIENDSHIP
INDEED

THAT DESK OF YOURS
HAD MAGIC IN IT
YOU WERE ABLE TO PULL
THINGS OUT OF IT
THAT NO ONE HAD SEEN

AND TWENTY SOME YEARS
IS A PRETTY LONG TIME

SO WHAT CAN WE SAY
OR WHAT CAN WE DO
TO GET YOU TO STAY
FOR ANOTHER
TWENTY SOME YEARS

AN INDIAN

AS I SIT
LOOKING AT ME
AN INDIAN
A WARRIOR
A CHIEF
ON A PIECE OF PAPER
NOT A MAN
BUT A MIRROR
CAN HE SEE ME
LYING
CHEATING
STEALING
I TOOK OVER
HIS LAND
HIS BUFFALO
HIS FREEDOM
IN RETURN
I GAVE HIM
A JUNK-YARD
MEDI-CAL
GOD BLESS AMERICA
LAND OF THE FREE
GOD BLESS AMERICA
HOW MUCH LONGER
CAN IT BE

STRONG LOVE

FOR WHAT WE LIVE IN

WAS MADE

FROM MANY TREES

TREES THAT ARE LOVE

FOR EVERY LEAF

THAT FALLS

ANOTHER IS SURE TO GROW

BIGGER AND STRONGER

THAN BEFORE

JUST LIKE OUR LOVE

FOUND LOVE

WHEN YOU TAKE ONES HAND

THAT HAND IS HELD CLOSE

CLOSE TO YOUR HEART

BECAUSE THE LOVE YOU
FOUND

HAS BEEN JOINED AT LAST

SO THIS IS YOUR DAY

AND IT IS YOUR TIME

TO REMEMBER

FOR THE REST OF YOUR LIVES

BECAUSE

FOUND LOVE

IS FOUND AT LAST

UNTOLD PATH

TODAY
WAS A DIFFERENT KIND
OF DAY

WHEN
I STARTED DOWN A PATH

WHERE I CAME UPON
A SOLDIER

HE WAS DOWN
ON HIS KNEES

AND
I COULD HEAR HIM

AS HE WAS PRAYING

AND
A TEAR
RAN DOWN HIS FACE

HE SAID
THAT HE WAS SORRY

BECAUSE HE
HAD LOST A FRIEND

AND
THAT HE WISHED
IT WAS HIM
INSTEAD

AND
HE SAID OUT LOUD

WHAT COULD I HAVE DONE

SO I KNELT BESIDE HIM

AS I PUT MY ARM AROUND HIM

TO COMFORT HIM
AND
THEN I WHISPERED
IN HIS EAR

WHAT IS DONE
IS DONE

YOU CAN NOT CHANGE
THE PAST

BUT YOU CAN
CHANGE THE FUTURE

SO TELL HIS STORY
ABOUT WHAT HE HAD DONE

AS A SOLDIER
AND
AS A FRIEND

THEN THE SOLDIER
STOOD UP

WIPED AWAY SOME TEARS

HE CLICKED HIS HEELS
THEN
SALUTED HIS BROTHER
HIS FRIEND

AND
THEN HE SAID

I WILL TELL THEM

OF
AN UNTOLD PATH

AND THEN
MY JOURNEY
CARRIED ME ON

TO A PLACE
WHERE
THEY WERE
UNLOADING A PLANE

AND
I CAME UPON
ANOTHER SOLDIER

ALL DRESSED IN CLASS

AND I HEARD SOME ONE
ASKED HIM

ABOUT HIS UNIFORM
AND
WHAT HIS DUTY WAS

AS A TEAR
RAN DOWN HIS FACE

HE SAID
MY DUTY HERE TODAY

IS HARDER THAN ANYTHING
I HAVE EVER DONE

I AM HERE
TO ESCORT A SOLDIER

A FALLEN HERO
HOME TODAY

WHERE
THEY WILL LAY HIM TO REST

YOU SEE
WE FOUGHT SIDE BY SIDE

AND
WE ALWAYS SAID

THAT IF WE DIED
WE WOULD DIE
SIDE BY SIDE

AN UNSPOKEN OATH

BUT
AS YOU CAN SEE

I AM STILL ALIVE

I FELT THAT
I HAD LET HIM DOWN

AS THEY UNLOADED
THE CASKET
FROM THE PLANE

THE SOLDIER
STARTED TO BREAK

SO I PUT MY ARM AROUND HIM

TO COMFORT HIM
AND
THEN I WHISPERED
IN HIS EAR

WHAT IS DONE
IS DONE

YOU CAN NOT CHANGE
THE PAST

BUT YOU CAN CHANGE
THE FUTURE

SO TELL HIS STORY

SSGT RALPH LEE BUTLER, JR.

ABOUT WHAT HE HAD DONE

AS A SOLDIER
AND
AS A FRIEND

THEN THE SOLDIER

WIPED AWAY SOME TEARS

HE CLICKED HIS HEELS
AND
SALUTED HIS BROTHER

AND HE SAID

I WILL TELL THEM
OF
AN UNTOLD PATH

SO THEN MY JOURNEY
CARRIED ME ON

TO THIS RESTING PLACE

THAT'S WHERE I SAW

A FULL BIRD COLONEL

HE WAS THEIR

TO SAY SOME WORDS
OF COMFORT

AND
SOME WORDS
OF PEACE

ABOUT THIS FALLEN HERO

AND HE SAID

I TOOK THIS SOLDIER
UNDER MY WING

I TREATED HIM
LIKE MY SON

I WATCHED HIM GROW

TO BECOME
A VERY FINE SOLDIER

HE WOULD GIVE UP HIS SHIRT
IF YOU NEEDED ONE

HE WOULD GIVE UP
ANYTHING
JUST TO HELP SOMEONE
ALONG THE WAY

THEN
THE COLONEL
STARTED TO BREAK

WHEN HE HEARD THE TAPS

AS A TEAR
RAN DOWN HIS FACE

SO I PUT MY ARM AROUND HIM

TO COMFORT HIM
AND
THEN I WHISPERED
IN HIS EAR

SIR

WHAT IS DONE
IS DONE

YOU CAN NOT CHANGE
THE PAST

BUT YOU CAN CHANGE
THE FUTURE

SO TELL HIS STORY

ABOUT WHAT HE HAD DONE

AS A SOLDIER
AND
AS A SON

THAT'S WHEN
HE TOOK THE FLAG

AND
PRESENTED IT

TO THE SOLDIERS WIFE

HE CLICKED HIS HEELS
AND SALUTED THEM

TO PAY HIS LAST RESPECTS

AND THIS
IS WHAT SHE SAID

AS THEY LAID ME TO REST

I REMEMBER WHEN

YOU PUT YOUR ARMS
AROUND ME

TO COMFORT ME
AND
THEN YOU WOULD WHISPER
IN MY EAR

SAYING
WHAT IS DONE
IS DONE

FOR WE CAN NOT CHANGE
THE PAST

BUT WE CAN CHANGE
THE FUTURE

SO YOUR WORDS
WILL ALWAYS BE HEARD

AND
YOUR ACTIONS
WILL ALWAYS BE FELT

ALL ACROSS THIS LAND
AS A SOLDIER
AND
AS A FRIEND

FOR THIS
IS YOUR STORY

OF
AN UNTOLD PATH

WRITTEN BY:
RALPH LEE BUTLER JR
"ROWDY"
FEBRUARY 23, 2010

A SIMPLE REMINDER

I LOVE YOU

MORE THAN WORDS

CAN SAY

THEY'RE MANY MILES

BETWEEN US

BUT WHEN

THE ROADS CROSS

I'LL BE HOME

BECAUSE

MY HEART

IS WITH YOU

AND YOU ALONE

A POCKET REMINDER

HE FOUGHT
FOR ALL
THE WRONG REASONS

HE RAN
IN ALL
THE WRONG WAYS

BUT SELF
IS SOON
TO BE GONE

AN IMAGE
NO LONGER
TO BE

SO BLESSED IS THE MAN
WHO EXCEPTS CHRIST
FOR WITHIN THIS
IS ETERNAL LIFE

A SCHOOL DAY TO
REMEMBER

IT WAS MONDAY MORNING
AND WE WERE IN CLASS

OUR TEACHER WALKED IN
AND WE STOOD
FOR A MOMENT OF SILENCE

THEN SOMEONE SAID A PRAY

THEN WE SAID
THE PLEDGE OF ALLEGENCE
TO THE FLAG

IT WAS TUESDAY MORNING
AND WE WERE IN CLASS

OUR TEACHER WALKED IN
AND WE STOOD
FOR A MOMENT OF SILENCE

AS OUR TEACHER TOOK THE
BIBLE
FROM THE TOP OF HER DESK
AND PUT IT AWAY

NO ONE SAID A PRAYER

BUT WE STILL SAID
THE PLEDGE OF ALLEGENCE
TO THE FLAG

IT WAS WENDSDAY MORNING
AND WE WERE IN CLASS

OUR TEACHER WALKED IN
AND WE STOOD
FOR A MOMENT OF SILENCE

AS OUR TEACHER TOOK THE
FLAG
FROM THE WALL

SHE FOLDED IT UP
AND PUT IT AWAY

NO ONE SAID A PRAYER

AND NO ONE SAID
THE PLEDGE OF ALLEGENCE
TO THE FLAG

WELL
IT WAS THURSDAY MORNING
AND WE WERE IN CLASS

OUR TEACHER WALKED IN
AND WE STOOD
FOR A MOMENT OF SILENCE

AS A TEAR RAN DOWN HER
FACE

SHE SAID

YOU DO NOT HAVE TO STAND
FOR A MOMENT OF SILENCE

YOU CAN NOT SAY PRAYER

AND WE ARE NOT ALOUD TO
SAY
THE PLEDGE OF ALLEGENCE
TO THE FLAG
IN THIS SCHOOL ANYMORE

SO NO ONE SAID A PRAYER

AND NO ONE SAID
THE PLEDGE OF ALLEGENCE
TO THE FLAG

WELL IT WAS FRIDAY MORNING
AND WE WERE IN CLASS

WITH THE NEW
ADMINISTRATION
AND PARENTS FROM AROUND

AS OUR TEACH WALKED IN
WITH OUR PRINCIPAL

ONE OF THE KIDS STOOD UP
AND ASKED THE MAN IN THE
SUIT
FOR A DOLLAR BILL

THEN HE ASKED A PARENT
FROM THE CROWED
FOR A DOLLAR BILL TOO

HE TOLD THEM
THAT THEY CAN HAVE IT BACK

SO THE LITTLE BOY
STOOD IN FRONT OF THE
CLASS
WITH THE DOLLAR BILLS

HE LICKED THEM
AND STUCK THEM
TO THE BOARD

HE WROTE BELOW ONE OF
THEM
IN GOD WE TRUST

THE OTHER HE WROTE
UNITED STATES OF AMERICA

THEN HIS TEACHER CAME UP
AND SHE WROTE
UNITED WE STAND

ALL STOOD THERE
IN A MOMENT OF SILENCE

AS THE BOY REACHED IN HER
DESK

HE PULLED OUT THE BIBLE
AND PLACED IT BACK
ON TOP OF HER DESK

THEN HE TOOK THE FLAG
AND PUT IT BACK
ON THE WALL

THEN SOMEONE FROM THE
CROWD
SAID A PRAYER
OUT LOUD

THEN EVERYONE SAID
THE PLEDGE OF ALLEGENCE
TO THE FLAG

WELL
IT WAS MONDAY MORNING
AND WE WERE IN CLASS

OUR TEACHER WALKED IN
AND WE STOOD
FOR A MOMENT OF SILENCE

THEN
SOMEONE SAID A PRAYER OUT
LOUD

THEN WE ALL
SAID THE PLEDGE OF
ALLEGENCE
TO THE FLAG

THIS WILL ALWAYS BE
A SCHOOL DAY TO REMEMBER

AS THE DOLLAR BILLS
REMAINED

AND ONE SAID
IN GOD WE TRUST

THE OTHER SAID
UNITED STATES OF AMERICA

AND IN BIG BOLD LETTERS
IT READ
UNITED WE STAND

STORMY SKYS

THERE IS A STORM
BUILDING TONIGHT

THERE IS A CLOUD
OF PAIN AND SUFFERING

THERE IS A STORM
BUILDING TONIGHT

THERE IS A CLOUD
OF FEAR AND SORROW

BUT BEFORE
THE STORM HITS

THERE WILL BE
UNEVEN SKYS TONIGHT

DON'T LET THE STORM
BUILD TOMORROW

SO TELL ME
THERE CAN BE PEACE
TONIGHT

THAT WE CAN FIX IT
BEFORE IT'S TO LATE

FOR THIS STORM WILL
ALWAYS BE REMEMBERED

IF WE DON'T FIX IT
TONIGHT

YOUR PICTURE & FRAME

I Want To Be
Your Picture

I Want To Be
Your Picture Frame

And In Your Picture
I Want It To Be
With Smiles
And Happy Memories

I Want To Be
Your Picture

I Want To Be
Your Picture Frame

And With The Strength
Of The Frame
I Will Hold Your Picture
And Embrace Your Memories

I Want To Be
Your Picture

I Want To Be
Your Picture Frame

ALL GAVE SOME
AND SOME GAVE ALL

I WAS JUST OUT
OF HIGH SCHOOL

AND
IT WAS TIME
TO GO

TO A PLACE
WE HEARD OF

AND
WE KNEW

WE MIGHT NOT
COME HOME

IT WAS FOR
OUR COUNRTY

SO WE TOOK A STAND

WITH MANT OTHERS
BY MY SIDE

YOU BECAME
MY BROTHERS

A FAMILY
AWAY FROM HOME

SO PLEASE
REMEMBER ME

IF I DID NOT
COME HOME

I HELD THAT LINE
JUST LIKE YOU

AS YOU COVERED
MY BACK
AND
WE PRAYED

PRAYING
AND
PRAYING

THAT WE WOULD ALL
MAKE IT BACK

SO IF YOU SEE ME
OR SEE MY NAME

ON THAT WALL

REMEMBER

ALL GAVE SOME
AND
SOME GAVE ALL

MY TRUCK DRIVING BUDDY

YOU'RE MY TRUCK
DRIVING BUDDY

YOU'RE MY TRUCK
DRIVING PAL

ITS NOT SO LONELY
WHEN I HAVE YOU HERE

THE TOUCH OF YOUR PAWS
AND
THE SOUND OF YOUR BARK

IT TELLS ME MANY THINGS
ABOUT THE WAY YOU CARE

YOU'RE MY TRUCK
DRIVING BUDDY

YOU'RE MY TRUCK
DRIVING PAL

WE PASS
THE TIME TOGETHER

CHASING EACH OTHER
RUNNING ABOUT

YOU WATCH ME
EVERY WHERE I GO

EVEN WHEN IM FUELING
YOU WATCH ME THREW THE
MIRRORS

WHEN ITS TIME TO REST
YOU CUDDLE UP CLOSE

YOU'RE MY TRUCK
DRIVING BUDDY

YOU'RE MY TRUCK
DRIVING PAL

SO I WONDER
WHEN I SEE YOU AT THE
WHEEL

LOOKING OVER THE DASH

I CAN HEAR YOU SAY

YOU'RE MY TRUCK
DRIVING BUDDY

YOU'RE MY TRUCK
DRIVING FRIEND

AND I WILL
ALWAYS BE

YOUR TRUCK DRIVING
BUDDY

YOUR TRUCK DRIVING
PAL

MY BROTHERHOOD

WHEN ONE FALLS
ALL WILL FALL

WHEN ONE RISES
ALL WILL RISE

ITS AN UNSPOKEN OATH
AN OATH
THAT WE LIVE BY
AND AN OATH
WE WILL DIE BY

BECAUSE
WE ARE BROTHERS
SIDE BY SIDE

SO I ASK YOU
MY FRIEND
ARE YOU WILLING
TO TAKE A STAND
FOR THE
RED, WHITE AND BLUE

BECAUSE
THIS IS MY BROTHERHOOD

GRANDPA'S LITTLE GIRL

YOUR HUGS
AND
YOUR KISSES
ARE HELD
DEEP IN MY HEART
BECAUSE
YOUR GRANDPA'S
LITTLE GIRL

I REMEMBER WHEN
I HERD THOSE WORDS
FOR THE VERY FIRST TIME

BOY OH BOY

YOU SAID IT OUT LOUD
AND VERY PROUD
"GRANDPA"
AND
YOU SAID IT
ON MY BIRTHDAY

A GIFT
THAT WOULD GROW
FROM THAT DAY ON

BUT
IT WAS SOMETHING
I WAS NOT READY FOR
AT THAT TIME

BUT
YOU DID GROW
DEEP IN MY HEART
BECAUSE
YOU ARE
GRANDPA'S LITTLE GIRL

AND AS YOU WERE
GROWING UP

MODELING YOUR CLOTHES
AND THINGS

YOU TOLD ME
THAT YOU WERE NOT
A LITTLE GIRL
ANYMORE
THAT YOU WERE
A BIG GIRL NOW

SO IN MY MIND
I KNEW IT WAS TRUE
BUT
IN MY HEART
I DIDN'T WANT TO LET GO
BECAUSE YOUR
GRANDPA'S LITTLE GIRL

BUT
SOME TIME AFTER
YOU CAME UP
AND SAT ON MY LAP
AND YOU ASKED ME
IF YOU WERE STILL
GRANDPA'S LITTLE GIRL

AND
I WAS PROUD
TO SAY
YES
YOU'RE MY LITTLE GIRL
AND THAT
YOU WILL ALWAYS BE
GRANDPA'S LITTLE GIRL

WELL THE LOOK
ON YOUR FACE
AND THE SMILE
YOU HAD
IT WAS LIKE CHRISTMAS
IN A CHILDS DREAM

SO I HOPE YOU KNOW
THAT I WILL BE THEIR
FOR YOU
EVEN WHEN
YOUR GROWN

SO REMEMBER THIS
WITH EVERY HUG
I GET
AND EVERY KISS
YOU GIVE
IT MAKES ME PROUD
TO BE YOUR GRANDPA
AND
TO HAVE YOU
AS MY GRANDAUGHTER

I HOPE YOU CAN SEE
THE SMILES
AND THE JOY
YOU PUT IN ME
WHEN I HERE THOSE WORDS
LIKE YOU DID
FOR THE VERY FIRST TIME

YOU SAID IT LOUD
AND
YOU SAID IT PROUD
AND
BECAUSE OF YOU
I TOO
WILL SAY IT LOUD
AND
SAY IT PROUD
WITH A TEAR
IN MY EYE
BECAUSE
YOUR GRANDPA'S LITTLE GIRL
AND
BECAUSE OF THE LOVE
I HAVE FOR YOU

I CAN WRITE THESE WORDS
AND NOT BE HURT
I CAN SHARE
THE WAY I FEEL
AND
PASS THIS ON TO YOU
BECAUSE
YOU ARE
GRANDPA'S LITTLE GIRL

A GIFT TO REMEMBER

IT ONLY COMES
ONCE A YEAR

A TIME OF LAUGHTER
AND
A TIME OF CHEER

BECAUSE
ITS CHRISTMAS

THE TIME OF YEAR
WE WILL REMEMBER
UNTIL NEXT YEAR

SO LAUGHT OUT LOUD
AND
SPRED YOUR CHEER

THIS
CHRISTMAS YEAR

WITH GIFTS
AND TREATS

EVERY THING SWEET

LIKE
HOME MADE CANDY
POUND CAKE
AND
PEAR PIE

SO ITS
HO HO HO

OH
WHAT A TREAT

A TIME LIKE THIS
ONLY COMES

ONCE A YEAR

SO STOP

AND PAUSE
FOR THE CAUSE

TAKE A LOOK
AT THE CHRISTMAS TREE

THE LIGHTS
AND ORINAMENTS

THEY SPEAK FOR THEMSELVES

PIECES OF HISTORY
TREW OUT THE YEARS

AND
DO NOT MINGEL
IN THOSE GIFTS

OR
SANTA
WILL NOT COME
FOR ANOTHER YEAR

THE GIRLS
ARE IN THE KITCHEN

COOKING UP THE DINNER

HOT ROLLS
TURKEY
AND HAM
AND
WHAT ABOUT THOSE
DEVILD EGGS

AND
A WHOLE LOT MORE

IM GLAD IT'S ONLY
ONCE A YEAR

BECAUSE
MY WAIST
CAN NOT HANDEL THIS
ALL YEAR ROUND

SO
THE GIFT I BRING
IS A HEART
OF LOVE
AND
A TEAR
OF JOY

TO BE WITH YOU
ON THIS CHRISTMAS DAY

HOPE YOU HAVE
A VERY
MERRY CHRISTMAS
THIS YEAR

LOVE DAD
2009

NUMBERS TO LETTERS

NUMBERS TO LETTERS
AND
LETTERS TO WORDS

WHEN WE MEET

IT WAS A SIX LETTER WORD
AND
THAT WAS A FRIEND

AND
TIME WENT ON

AND
WE BECAME
A TEN LETTER WORD

AND
IT WAS FRIENDSHIP

WELL OUR FRIENDSHIP
BECAME
A FOUR LETTER WORD

AND
THAT WAS LOVE

IT WAS NEVER BUILT

ON A THREE LETTER WORD

IT WAS ALL BUILT
ON A SIX LETTER WORD

AND
WE BECAME ONE

IN A EIGHT LETTER WORD

AND
THAT IS MARRIAGE

AND
YOU HAVE BECOME
MY FOUR LETTER WORD

TWO TIMES OVER

MY WIFE

MY LOVE

A VETERAN

I PROUDLY SERVED
MY COUNTRY

I DID ALL
THAT I COULD DO

TO PROTECT HER
AND
TO KEEP HER FREE

EVEN THOUGH
I NO LONGER SERVE

IN ANY BRANCH
OF THE SERVICE

LIKE THE MARINES
THE AIR FORCE
THE ARMY
OR THE NAVY

I WILL ALWAYS BE
A VETERAN

BECAUSE I SERVED
IN ONE OF THESE

AND
YOU CAN SEE

OTHER VETERANS
LIKE ME

THAT ARE PROUD

PROUD TO BE
AN AMERICAN

PROUD
TO BE FREE

WE FLY
OUR COLORS
WITH PRIDE

BECAUSE
WE ARE VETERANS

PROUD
OF THIS GREAT LAND

AND WE WILL
DEFEND HER
EVEN TO THIS DAY

BECAUSE WE ARE
VETERANS

THAT TOOK AN OATH
TO KEEP HER FREE

SO REMEMBER
IF YOU LOVE YOUR FREEDOM
THANK A VETERAN

BECAUSE
THEY SHED THEIR BLOOD
FOR YOU AND ME
JUST
TO KEEP HER FREE

A FIGHTING PRAYER

I WILL FIGHT
THIS FIGHT

WITH
EVERY STEP
I TAKE

AND
EVERY STRIDE
I MAKE

FOR
EVERY MILE
I GO

I WILL PRAY
FOR HOPE

BECAUES
I CARRY A PRAYER

A PRAYER OF HOPE

EVERY WHERE
I GO

SO TAKE MY HAND

AND
TOGETHER

WE WILL STAND

IN THIS BATTLE OF HOPE

THEN WE CAN
SAY OUT LOUD

FOR
EVERY STEP

WE TAKE

AND
EVERY STRIDE
WE MAKE

FOR
EVERY MILE
WE GO

WE WILL PRAY

A PRAYER
FOR HOPE

BECAUSE
OF YOUR FIGHT

AND
THE INSPIRATION
YOU SHOW

YOU WILL ALWAYS BE

IN MY MIND
AND
IN MY HEART

KNOW MATTER
WHERE WE GO

WRITTEN BY;
"ROWDY"
RALPH LEE BUTLER JR.

A JOURNEY

A JOURNEY
HAS MANY VOICES

IT TELLS
A TAIL

OF
MANY TRAILS

SO
THE JOURNEY
I TRAVEL

IS A JOURNEY
UNTOLD

SO
IN MY JOURNEY

I WILL FIND
A STORY

THAT CAN BE TOLD

SO
IF YOU TRAVEL

DOWN THIS JOURNEY

YOU WILL HEAR
MY VOICE

THAT TELLS
A TAIL

ABOUT
THIS TRAIL

OF
MY JOURNEY

UNNAMED HEROES

YOU'RE THE ONES

THAT STOOD
IN THE SHADOWS

THE SHADOWS
OF THE DARK

WHILE OTHERS RAN OUT

YOU WERE THERE

RUSHING IN

TO TAKE CARE
OF OUR FALLEN

FOR THIS
IS THE SPIRIT
AND
THE PRIDE

OF
OUR UNNAMED HEROES

FOR THE RISK
YOU TAKE

YOU NEVER DO
HESITATE

BECAUSE
YOU RISK IT ALL

JUST TO SAVE A LIFE

SOME OF US
STOOD THERE

ON SEPT. 11TH.

WE SAW
WHAT WAS TAKEN

AND
WE COULD NOT BELEAVE
OUR EYES

AS OUR HEARTS FELL
TO OUR KNEES

AND TEARS
RAN DOWN OUR FACE

BECAUSE
WE WERE
UNDER ATTACK

AND THEN
SOME UNNAMED HEROES

RUSHED IN

TO GIVE US HOPE

HOPE FOR TOMORROW

THAT WE COULD STAND
HERE TODAY

SIDE BY SIDE
AND
HAND IN HAND

KNOWING THAT
OUR FLAG

WILL STILL
SHINE THROUGH

THOSE DARK FILLED SKIES

AS THE UNNAMED HEROES

HELPED
YOU AND ME

FOR WE WILL REMEMBER
SEPT. 11TH.

AS NINE ELEVEN

AND
THE CALL OF 911

WHEN
FLIGHT 11
HIT THE NORTH TOWER
AT 8:45

THE CALL WENT OUT

AS THE UNNAMED HEROES

CAME TO OUR AID

RUSHING IN

JUST TO HELP
THOSE IN NEED

AND THEN
IT HIT AGAIN

FLIGHT 175
HIT THE SOUTH TOWER
AT 9:05

TWO OTHER FLIGHTS

TOOK A TOLL

FLIGHT 77
THAT HIT THE PENTAGON
AT 9:39

THEN FLIGHT 93
THAT CRASHED AT 10:03

YES
THIS IS A TIME

FOR ALL OF US
TO PAUSE

AND
TO REMEMBER

WHEN THE WORLD
STOOD STILL

ON
SEPT. 11TH. 2001

AS MEN AND WOMEN

FROM ALL AROUND

CAME TO OUR AID

AND
EVEN TO THIS DAY

I SEE YOU THERE

WAITING

WAITING
IN THE SHADOWS

WILLING
TO MAKE A SACRIFCE

JUST TO HELP SOMEONE

AT ANY GIVEN TIME

BECAUSE YOU ARE

THE UNNAMED HEROES

TO THE CALL

OF 911

BECAUSE OF YOU

AND
YOUR SACRAFICE

WE ARE ABLE

TO STAND HERE
TODAY

SIDE BY SIDE
AND
HAND IN HAND

KNOWING THAT
SOME UNNAMED HEROES

WILL ALWAYS
COME TO OUR AID

AND
BECAUSE OF YOU

AND
YOUR PRIDE

WE CAN SEE THOSE COLORS

LIKE
RED, WHITE, AND BLUE

FOR THESE
ARE THE COLORS

THAT RUN

IN UNNAMED HERO
LIKE YOU

When Soldiers Meet

You have heard
My words
And
You have seen
My patch

For we went
As strangers
And
We came home
As brothers

For as uneak
As it might be

It is
So very true

For those
Who served

Because
We will always remember
Another brother

And
Even to this day

When soldiers meet

Past and present

They too
Will become
A brother

Because of the pride
And
The respect we have
For one another

It is sure to glow
Deep
Within our souls

For this
Is the first time

I have seen him
And
He stood before me

An officer
And
A gentlemen

Then
He saluted me

An NCO

In that little café

Just down the road

And as a soldier
I too
In return
Saluted him
An officer

With pride
And respect

Then
We hugged one another

As brothers do

PDA
Didn't mean a thing

And
Others from around

Saw the respect
And
The reflection

Of our brotherhood

That's when a stranger
Came up
From across the room

And asked us
About our service

Because
He too had served

And
Had seen the pride

That shined through
The both of us

We were proud to say

Yes
We have served
Our country

But not with each other

But it would have been
Such a great honor

To have served
With one another

So we shared some things
With this soldier

And
As he left

He left
As brother

So as it stands

The major
Once again

Saluted me
An NCO
As we parted our ways

Oh what an honor

It felt that day

When we meet
In that little cafe

So
This will always be

Something
I will remember

For this
Is something
That is unheard of

Something
That is unseen

When an officer
Salutes a soldier

But this
Was among brothers

For the respect

That we have
For one another

So as it remains

We meet as strangers
And
Parted as brothers

So I saluted you

Not only
As an officer

But
As my brother

With pride
And respect

From one soldier
To another

For this is a bond
That can not be broken

And
This is an oath
That is not spoken

For this
Is respect
From one another

Only
When Soldiers Meet

A HUNTERS DREAM

IT ALL STARTS
ON OPENING DAY

AT THE BREAK
OF DAWN

SITTING
UP IN A DEER STAND

OUT ALONG THE TREES

IN THE BITTER COLD

IN THE FOG

RAIN OR SNOW

LOOKING
FOR THAT MONSTER BUCK

A DREAM

THAT I WILL REMEMBER
FOR YEARS TO COME

WITH A BUCK
LIKE THIS

I WILL HAVE
A STORY TO TELL

FOR
I'LL REMEMBER

WHEN THE SUN CAME UP

AT THE BREAK OF DAWN

JUST UP
OVER THE HORIZON

AS THE SOUNDS
FROM ALL AROUND

START TO COME ALIVE

AS THE BIRDS
STARTED TO CHIRP

AND
THE CROWS FLEW BY

I SAW SOME DUCKS

CIRCLING AROUND

JUST BEFORE THEY LANDED
IN THE POND

YOU CAN HEAR THE TURKEYS
OFF IN THE DISTANCE

AS THEY COME
FROM THEIR ROOST

YOU CAN HEAR THEM

AS THEY
HIT THE GROUND

AND
YOU CAN HEAR

THE SOUNDS OF NATURE
FROM ALL AROUND

AS IT ALL
COMES ALIVE

IN THE MORNING
AT THE BREAK OF DAWN

AND
OFF IN THE DISTANCE

YOU CAN SEE

A DEER OR TWO
AND
A LITTLE BUCK
THAT IS RUNNING
WITH SOME DOES

ACTING LIKE HE'S THE BOSS

THEN OUT OF NOWHERE

THEIR HE STOOD

THE MONSTER

THE DREAM
OF ALL TIMES

STANDING
IN THE SUN LIGHT

WITH A RACK SO BIG
AND
SO TALL

HIS BODY
STANDING LIKE
A KING

FOR HE IS THE PRIDE
OF
THE DEER I SEE

AS MY HEART
STARTS POUNDING

LOUDER THAN ANY DRUM

IT'S BEATING SO HARD
AND SO FAST

AS MY BREATH
IS TAKEN AWAY

AS HE STANDS THEIR
IN THE PERFECT SOLOWET

AND THEN
BEFORE I COULD DO
ANYTHING

HE IF OFF
LIKE A GHOST

SO
THE DREAM

OF
THAT MONSTER BUCK

SHALL LIVE AGAIN

UNTIL THE DAWN
OF
ANOTHER DAY

I CAN ONLY DREAM
AS
I HAVE SEEN HIM

CRAWL
ACROSS THE OPEN FIELDS

FOR THE WEATHER
HAS BEEN
IN HIS FAVOR

TIME AND TIME AGAIN

AND

ONCE AGAIN
I SAW HIM THEIR

SO
I DREW BACK MY BOW
AND
I CAUGHT THE WIND
JUST RIGHT

I TRIED TO HOLD BACK
BUT
I JUST HAD TO LET GO

AND
SO I DID

AS I SNEEZED
NOT ONCE
OR
TWICE
BUT THREE TIMES
I DID

I JUST COULDN'T
HOLD IT BACK

AND
OFF HE WENT

BLOWING
AND
SNORTING AT ME

FROM
OFF INTO THE TREE LINE

AS
THIS LEGION LIVES ON

UNTIL THE NEXT TIME
WE MEET

SSGT RALPH LEE BUTLER, JR.

AND
AS SURE AS IT WAS

ANOTHER DAY
DID ARISE

I DREW BACK MY BOW

AS HE CAME OUT
FROM THE CEADER TREES

HE WAS
RUBBING THE BRANCHES

AND
LEAVING HIS MARK

HE WAS STANDING THEIR

SO BIG
AND
SO TALL

I WAITED UNTIL
HE TOOK
HIS LAST STEP

AS
THE ARROW FLEW
FROM
MY FINGER TIPS

UP AND OVER
MY ARROW HE JUMP

AND AGAIN

OFF INTO THE TREE LINE
HE WENT

BLOWING
AND

SNORTING AT ME
ONCE AGAIN

I JUST THOUGHT
TO MYSELF

IT COULD NOT BE TRUE
I HAD HIM

THE TROPHY
OF A HUNTERS DREAM

BUT AS IT WAS

A LEGION SO TRUE
AND BOLD

FOR
HE WILL LIVE AGAIN

UNTIL ANOTHER DAY

BUT I WILL REMEMBER

THAT I HAD
MY CHANCE
TWO TIMES ALREADY
THIS YEAR

YES
IT'S ALL BEEN
IN HIS FAVOR

BUT
I WAS SURE

THE THIRD TIME
WOULD BE A CHARM

THAT'S
WHEN HE WOULD FALL

AS HIS LUCK
WAS SURE TO RUN OUT

WHEN RIFLE SEASON
WOULD COME ABOUT

I WOULD BE THEIR

UP IN A TREE

WAITING FOR HIM

YOU KNOW
THAT BIG MONSTER BUCK

AND
AS IT WAS

HIS LUCK
JUST RAN OUT

AS I SAW HIM
STANDING THEIR

RIGHT IN FRONT OF ME

NOT EVEN 30 YARDS

SO I RAISED MY RIFLE
VERY SLOW

AS
I TOOK MY AIM

TELLING MYSELF

TO
BREATH IN
BREATH OUT

AS MY HEART
WAS POUNDING

LIKE THE DRUMS
AT A POW WOW

I PULLED THE TRIGGER
AND
THE HAMMER FELL

ONCE AGAIN

HE DID NOT FALL

JUST OFF
INTO THE TREE LINE
HE WENT

SNORTTING AT ME

AS
IF HE WAS LAUGHING

BLOWING
AND
PAWING
AT THE GROUND

JUST LIKE BEFORE

BUT I STILL

COULD NOT BELIEVE

WHAT HAD HAPPENED

OVER
AND OVER

I THOGHT TO MYSELF

WHAT DID I DO WRONG

I KNOW
I LOADED MY RIFLE

SSGT RALPH LEE BUTLER, JR.

I KNOW
I PUT ONE IN THE CHAMBER

I KNOW
I TOOK THE SAFETY OFF

SO WHAT
WENT WRONG

TRYING
NOT TO SECOND GUEST
MYSELF

AS I CHAMBERED
ANOTHER ROUND

THAT'S WHEN I FOUND

THAT THE ROUND
HAD MISFIRED

SO ONCE AGAIN

LUCK
WAS ON HIS SIDE
ONCE MORE

BUT
I WILL ALWAYS REMEMBER

WHEN I HAD
MY CHANCE

AT
THAT MONSTER BUCK

FOR SOME
WILL NEVER SEE
OR
GET A SHOT

AT A MONSTER BUCK
LIKE HIM

BUT ONLY
IN THEIR DREAMS

SO
I WILL TRY AGAIN

WHEN THE SEASON
OPENS AGAIN
NEXT YEAR

AS
I CAN HEAR
THAT BUCK

THE MONSTER BUCK

TELL HIS OWN STORY

ABOUT
HOW HE SURVIVED
ANOTHER HUNTING SEASON

IN MY BACK YARD

AND
THAT HE
WILL BE LOOKING FOR ME

ON OPENING DAY
AT THE BREAK OF DAWN

FOR
I'M THE HUNTER
HE HAS NOT SEEN

SITTING
SOMEWHERE
IN THE TREES

FOR HE
WILL ALWAYS BE
LOOKING FOR ME

AS IM LOOKING
FOR HIM

AND
HE WILL REMAIN

THE MONSTER BUCK

THE GLIMPSE
OF
A HUNTERS DREAM

A SOLDIERS TREE

SOME OF YOU
MIGHT CALL THIS
A CHRISTMAS TREE

AND OTHERS
MIGHT CALL IT
AN ANGEL TREE

BUT I
WILL CALL IT
A SOLDIERS TREE

AND
IT GOES LIKE THIS

IT WAS ABOUT A WEEK
BEFORE CHRISTMAS

WHEN I HEARD
THE SOLDIERS TALKING

TALKING ABOUT CHRISTMAS

ABOUT BEING AWAY
FROM THEIR FAMILYS
AND
THEIR FRIENDS
THIS YEAR

THEY WHERE TALKING ABOUT
THE TREES
THE LIGHTS
AND
THE ORNAMENTS

THE GIFTS
AND
TREATS

ABOUT THE GATHERING
OF FRIENDS

WITH THE LAUGHTER
OF JOY
AND PEACE

AND A WHOLE LOT
OF OTHER THINGS

SO AS I WALKED ON BY

I KNEW
RIGHT THEN AND THEIR

AS IT ALL STARTED
TO SOAK ON IN

I THOGHT ABOUT
THE STORY OF JESUS

BEING BORN
ON CHRISTMAS DAY

I KNEW RIGHT THEN
WITH OUT A DOUGHT

THAT I HAD A MISSION

AND ONCE AGAIN

I'D SEE IT THROGHT
TO THE END

SO OFF I WENT

DOWN TO THE SUPPLY ROOM

TO SEE THE SUPPLY SGT.

WITH JUST A SMALL REQUEST

IT WAS FOR SOME WIRE
AND A BROOM HANDLE

ABOUT 4 FEET TALL

TO BE THE POLL
THE BASE OF A TREE

FOR THIS WAS MY PLAN
THAT I HAD IN MIND
AS THE SGT
ANSWERED MY CALL
LIKE A GRENCH WOULD DO

FOR HE LAUGHT OUT LOUD
AT THIS REQUEST

HE TOLD ME
THAT IT WOULD NOT WORK

NO MATTER
WHAT I WOULD DO

BUT
HE GAVE IT TO ME ANYWAY

AND OFF I WENT
TO THINK AND PRAY
ABOUT WHAT I CAN DO

SO DOWN TO THE MESS HALL
I WOULD GO

JUST TO RELAX
WITH A CUP OF COFFEE
OR TWO

JUST TO SIT
AND THINK AWHILE

AS I DREW IT UP
ON A PIECE OF PAPER

THAT I HAD

FOR I KNEW
RIGHT THEN

IT WAS GOING TO BE
LIKE A CHARLIE BROWN TREE

BUT
IT WAS GOING TO HAVE TO DO

THAT'S WHEN A SOLDIER
FROM OUT OF NO WHERE
JUST APPEARED

HE WAS STANDING
NEXT TO ME

AND HE SAW
WHAT I WAS TRYING TO DOING

SO I TOLD HIM
ABOUT MY MEN

ABOUT THEIR STORIES
THEY HAD HAD

TALKING ABOUT
CHRISTMAS TREES
BEING SO BIG
AND TALL

ALL FULL OF LIFE
AS THEY STARTED TO GLOW

THEN THIS SOLDIER
WANTED TO HELP
BUILD THIS TREE

HE TOLD ME
TO USE SOME PAPER
TO COVER THE LIMBS

IT WOULD MAKE THIS TREE
BLOOM RIGHT ON OUT

BUT I TOLD HIM
I HAD NO GLUE OR TAPE

AND HE SAID
JUST HAVE SOME FAITH
AND IT WILL DO

MIXED TOGETHER
SOME FLOUR AND WATER

IT WOULD MAKE A PASTE
AND ACT LIKE GLUE

RIGHT THEN
THAT OLD GRENCH
FROM SUPPLY
STARTED IN
ONCE AGAIN

LAUGHING AT ME
ABOUT MY TREE

FOR I DID NOT KNOW
THAT HE WAS THERE

IN THE MESS HALL
LISTENING
TO WHAT I HAD SAID
OUT LOUD

IT WAS AS IF
I WAS PRAYING
OR JUST TALKING TO MYSELF

SO I TOLD MYSELF
THAT WAS IT

FOR I COULDN'T TAKE NO
MORE

SSGT RALPH LEE BUTLER, JR.

FROM THAT OLD GRENCH

SO I YELLED OUT

YOUR AN OLD GROUCH
AND YOUR JUST LIKE
A GRENCH

WHY DON'T YOU GET
SOME CHRISTMAS SPIRIT
AND
HAVE A LITTLE FAITH

BECAUSE THESE SOLDIERS
STILL HAVE A DREAM
AND
SOME KIND OF PRAYER
FOR CHRISTMAS
THIS YEAR

AND BECAUSE OF THAT
IM DOING MY BEST
TO SEE IT THROUGH

SO OFF HE WENT
NOT A WORD WAS SAID

THAT'S WHEN THIS SOLDIER
STILL STANDING NEXT TO ME

TOLD ME
TO COOL MY JETS

THAT THIS
WOULD ALL WORK OUT

WITH A SIMPLE PRAYER
OF FAITH
AND HOPE

AND FOR THAT GRENCH
YOU SAY

LET ME TELL YOU
SOMETHING
ABOUT THAT MAN

YOU SEE
HE LOST HIS SON
A FEW YEARS BACK
ON CHRISTMAS EVE

AND LIKE SO MANY

THEY LOOSE THEIR FAITH
AND HAVE NO HOPE

THAT IS WHY
THEY ACT LIKE THEY DO

BUT THEN
SOMEONE COMES ALONG
LIKE YOU

THAT HELPS
RESTORE THEIR FAITH
AND
GIVES THEM HOPE ONCE
MORE

THEN HE ASKED ME

IF I REMEMBERED
THE G.I. JOES

THAT HUNG ON THE WALL
DOWN IN SUPPLY

I TOLD HIM I DID
AND
THIS IS WHAT HE SAID

FOR THOSE LITTLE G. I. JOES
THAT HANG ON THE WALL

THEY REMIND HIM
OF HIS SON

A SOLDIER TOO

YOU SEE
HIS SON ONCE TOLD HIM
ALONG TIME AGO
THAT HE WAS LIKE
THE G.I. JOE

FOR THESE ARE MY HEROES
JUST LIKE YOU

SO EVEN THOUGH
THEY HANG ON THE WALL

THEY ARE A REFLECTION
OF HIS SON

FOR THEY
ARE LIKE ANGELS

THAT HIS SON
HELD ON TO

WELL
A COUPLE OF DAYS HAD
PASSED
AND
THE TREE WAS DONE

IT LOOKED
A LITTLE PLANE JANE

BUT FAITH
AND HOPE
DID COME TRUE

THAT'S
WHEN OUT OF NOW WHERE

THEIR HE CAME
THE SGT FROM THE SUPPLY

NOT TO SURE WHAT TO SAY
OR EVEN DO

BUT I STOOD BEFORE HIM
TALL AND PROUD
AND I SAID OUT LOUD
SEMPER-FI

FOR YOUR SON
WOULD BE PROUD

FOR THE ITEMS YOU GAVE

TO HELP MAKE
THIS SOLDIERS TREE

FOR THIS
WILL RESTORE
SOME SOLDIERS FAITH
AND
GIVE THEM HOPE
ON CHRISTMAS EVE

THAT'S WHEN
HE TURNED
AS WHITE AS GHOST
AND
HE SAID OUT LOUD

WITH EXCITEMENT
IN HIS VIOCE

I WILL BE RIGHT BACK
SO PLEASE
DON'T GO
AND DO NOT DO
ANY THING
TO THAT TREE

AND
WHEN HE CAME BACK

HE HAD A SACK
FULL OF WASHER
AND CAN OF PAINT

O D GREEN
IF YOU KNOW WHAT I MEAN

HE SAID OUT LOUD
WITH A WHOLE LOT OF PRIDE

YOU CAN PAINT THIS TREE
IN A MILITARY GREEN

YOU CAN HANG THE WASHER
LIKE ORNIMENTS WOULD
HANG

JUST LIKE
MY SON AND I
ONCE DID

I TRIED TO THANK HIM
FOR ALL THAT HE DONE

AS HE STARTED TO LEAVE
AND HE SAID
PLEASE
DON'T THANK ME
THANK HIM

AND READ MY NOTE
THEN PASS IT ON

MAKE SURE
YOU OPEN THIS BOX
ON CHRISTMAS EVE
AND
YOU WILL FIND
A G.I. JOE

THAT YOU CAN PUT
ON TOP OF YOUR TREE

FOR THIS
IS AN ANGLE
JUST LIKE MY SON
THAT IS STANDING
NEXT TO YOU

FOR HE
RESTORED OUR FAITH
AND GAVE US HOPE

AND AS I TURNED

THE SOLDIER WAS GONE
IN A BLINK OF AN EYE

SO I READ ON

THANK THE LORD
THIS CHRISTMAS EVE
FOR SENDING AN ANGEL
THAT STOOD NEXT TO ME

WHO HELPED US MAKE
THIS SOLDIERS TREE

ALL WAS DONE
BUT ONE REQUEST

SO WE GATHERED AROUND
ON CHRISTMAS EVE

AND THAT G. I. JOE
WAS PLACED
ON TOP OF THE TREE

AND AS WE DID

IT STARTED TO GLOW
FOR THIS

WAS THE TOY
THAT HIS SON
HELD ON TO

FOR IT IS AN ANGEL

THAT KEPT HIM SAFE

DAY AND NIGHT

BUT NOW IT SITS
ON A SOLDIERS TREE

EVEN IN MY DREAMS

WHEN I SEE YOU THERE
IT BRINGS BACK
SO MANY MEMORIES
WHEN I SEE YOU THERE
OH DARLING
WHEN I SEE YOU THERE
IT BRINGS JOY
AND PEACE
TO MY HEART
AND TO MY SOUL
FOR THIS IS MY LIFE
WHEN I SEE YOU THERE
EVEN
WHEN I CLOSE MY EYES
I SEE YOU THERE
STANDING
STANDING IN THE PERFECT
SILHOUETTE
WHEN I SEE YOU THERE
EVERYWHERE I LOOK
AND EVERYTHING I SEE
IT MAKES ME THINK OF YOU
BECAUSE IT IS YOU AND ME
SO EVERYWHERE I GO
AND EVERYTHING I DO
I SEE YOU THERE
HOLDING ME
EVERYWHERE
EVEN IN MY DREAMS

GOING HOME

There was a day
There was a time
When we stood
All together
At family gatherings
And things
But today
Is so much different
From those days
And tears will fall
As we gather here today
There was a day
There was a time
When we stood
Side by side
We saluted your brother
My father in-law
A Veteran of WWll
As they laid him to rest
And now
Here I am
Standing here
But not alone
To honor you
Another WWII Veteran
As they lay you to rest
With your brother
By my side
We too salute you
And he will lead you home
To be reunited
With other family members
And Vets.
So
There will be a day
And
There will be a time
When
We will all gather again
When
We're going home JORDON

Let her spirit soar
On the wings
Of an eagle
And
Let her love
Shine on me
For the doves we see
It will always be
Just you and me
My baby girl

THE PICTURE I CARRY

For the picture
I carry
It is a reminder
Of
My baby
That I carried
With-in me
For
The time
That we shared
With
Each other
Is now
A memory
That I carry
Not
In my body
But
In my heart
And
In my soul
For this
Was
My baby
My son
A picture
Of him
That I carry

TO MY BABY GIRL

This is not
A poke
or
Even a joke.
It has
two hands
and
It has
two arms
but
If you look close
you will see
they are wrapped
around you,
with love
and
tender care.
For this
Is a hug
that says
More than words
For this
Is an action
That says
I love you,
Love Dad

ITS JUST A STORY

Every story
Has
A beginning
And
Every beginning
Has
An ending
For
Every story
Has
A chapter
And
Every chapter
Has
A page
For
Every story
Has
A cover
And
Every cover
Has
A book
So
Read between the lines
And
You will find
Your
Own story
Deep
With in your book

MAY THE STORY NEVER END:
JUST LET IT SHINE
FROM WITHIN.

HOLD THOSE WORDS

If your heart
Burns with fire
You will speak
With flames
As sparks fly
from your mouth
So it is better
To bite your tong
Than to
Let the words
Out in fire
Take the time
And
Drink a glass
Of water
Let your heart soak
But
Not in sorrow
For then
Your words
Shall flow
In peace
Like
The rivers water

NO REGRETS

Life in it's self,
will help those
Who help others
Then
And only then
Will you see
The life of others
For this
We will glow
And friendship
Will shine
As the sun will rise
From the east
Then we can rest
As it settles
To the west
Until another day
Remember the words
That are spoken today
For its a start
Of a new beginning

THE START OF A DREAM

When I close my eyes
I see the things
from today
And as I dream
I dream of things
From yesterday
But tomorrow
As I wake
And open my eyes
This will be
A memory
A thing
Of the past
As I rest
My weary eyes
My body and soul
And I will start again
When I close my eyes

SSGT RALPH LEE BUTLER, JR.

Standing not alone

It is better
To stand
With a friend
In the darkness
Than to stand alone
Threw the light
For a friend
Will guide you
And you for him
So in the light
We can share
Whatever we found
In the darkness
For the glory
Of the things
We see
It will be felt
Not only
in the darkness
But in the light
as well
When you stand
With a friend
The darkness
Will cast a shadow
Into the light
Because we stood together
Threw thick and thin
For it is better
To stand
With a friend
In the darkness
Than to stand alone
Threw the light
Because no one
Can stand alone
If you want
A friend for life

THE ROAD TO 101

It all starts
Out here
On a road
To Hwy 101
From
The dirt roads
Back roads
And
City streets
Were they all
Come to meet
With
Country boys
And
City slickers
And
Let's not forget
about
Those wanna be's
Its just a way of life
As we travel
The different kinds
Of roads
This is what we'll learn
On the path
To the Hwy of 101
From the mountains
To the valley
All the way
To the open plains
For the path
We travel
Its just the way
To a Hwy of 101
Its destination
Is the middle
Of now where
A place
Of peace
And joy

As we travel
Our way
Down the one way path
There is no turning back
As we travel
The path
Of our own life
We can only change
The things ahead
As we travel
The Hwy of 101

THE WAY WE FEEL

Some of us
Can write
About the things
That we feel

While others
Just hide
Behind the things
That they feel

So they too
Will not be hurt
From the things
That they feel

With out ever
Speaking a word
About the things
That they feel

As we close our eyes
And walk away
From the things
That we feel

But still yet
The things
That we feel
Are still their

As they remain
In our hearts
And in our minds
Forever

And let us not forget
The ones that deny
The things
That they feel

Because
They are still
The things
That we feel....

ONE SEED

Some people
carry a seed
In there pocket
Some people
carry a seed
In there jeans
While others
carry a seed
In there hearts
But others
will only see it grow
And
they will nurture it
Along the way
As it grows
While others
can only dream
a dream
Of something
they never seen grow
So
if I ever
Planted a seed
Would I ever
see it grow
For it's never
to late
To see
what has grown
From a seed
that I carried
In my heart
and
in my soul

The Spirit Of A Wolf

I am the spirit
Of a wolf
For the light
Will shine
As my spirit
Shines on
Look not
Into my eyes
But look
For the shadows
And you will see
My silhouette
As it glows
From the mountain tops
And you shall find
Peace in your heart
As my spirit howls
At the moonlight

A REFLECTION OF COURAGE

For The Courage
I Have
And The Courage
You See
You Will See
A Reflection
Of Me

HONOR

To honor those
Who honored us
Is an honor
In its self
So to serve
Is an honor
An honor
That lives
Within myself

FRIENDS

Friends
are like
a dime a dozen
But those
who you think
Are your friends
Are just people
You know
But a true friend
Only comes
once
in a life time
For they
are the ones
That will stand
Next to you
Through thick and thin
No matter what
For they
will make sure
Your not alone
In good times
And in bad
For they
May be a friend
You really
never knew
You had
So share
These words
With a friend
You think
you know
And you will see
If that friend
Is a dime a dozen
Or one of the ones
That comes
Only once
in a life time

For these
are the friends
You really
want to know

THE MIRROR

For this
I can see
For that
I will be
But this
Is an image
Of me
So what
Do you see

From a Father To His Son

For I
am the pride
And you
are my cub
I am
the strength
And you
are the young
I am
your father
And you
Are my son
For I
am the king
Soon to be
A memory
Then you will be
The pride
Of what you see
And then
You will have
Your own cub

TO DREAM

To dream
is to dream
but to live a dream
is a dream
all in it's self.
so never give up
on your dreams,
because they
are alive and well.
for they
will give you hope
and inspiration
even when you dream
out loud.
but you'll never now
where your dreams
may lead you
until
you have lived
a dream
that you
have dreamed
yourself

WORDS OF ACTIONS

For the words
I speak
Are the action
Untold
But
The actions
Untold
Are the words
I speak

YOUR MIND AND HEART

Your Mind
Is Like A Picture
It Has
A Thousand Words To Tell
But
Your Heart
Has Many More
To Share

MY CHOICE

ONE VOICE,
ONE WORD,
ONE PERSON,
AND
ONE ACTION
FOR THIS WILL BE
AN EXPERIENCE
THAT WILL LAST
A LIFETIME

For
the words you see
And
the words you hear
They are twisted
For they are twisted
In this world
For a reason
So it leaves it up to you
To go figure things out
And to make sense of it all
In your mind
And in your heart.
For this is the power
That comes from with in yourself. So
set your mind
And your heart
To the things you want to achieve And
remember
To look for the light
At the end of the tunnel,
So when you finish
What you had started
You will find a pot of gold
At the end of the rainbow
That is waiting for you
Only when you achieve
What you set out to achieve.
So remember
No matter how hard

It might be
Tell your self
I can
And
I will
Be successful
Achieve my goals.
For I
am a special person
Because
I made it
to the end.
And for this
I am a winner
And no one
Owes me anything
But myself.

A TALK WITH GOD

I TALKED TO GOD TODAY
AND
HE ASKED ME
How Long
Will I Keep You
In My Life.
I Smiled
And Said:
How Do I
Choose Between
Forever
And
Always....

A MOTHERS LOVE

A mothers love
Is forever
Neither far
Or near
She will always
be there
Not only in body
But in spirit
And soul
Through the wind
And air
I will breath
My mothers air
And I can hear
her whisper
Threw the air
As she would say
I love you dear

LET MY VOICE BE HEARD

Let my voice
be heard
Not only
threw the night
But
threw the day
as well
From the shadows
of the dark
To the silhouette
of the moon
Let my voice
be heard

The magic of friendship

The magic
of friendship
Will start with
Is a sprinkle
Of joy
A pinch
Of happiness
And a sparkle
In our eyes
As our hearts beat
With tenderness
And our words
Are soft spoken
With purity
And meaning
So when we meet
For the very first time
I will see you smile
As I open my arms
And
I say to you
Welcome my friend
Welcome to my home
And family
For this
Is the magic of friendship
That I pass on to you

SOMETHING TO TELL

A picture tells
many stories
It has a thousand words
to tell
So let your mind wonder
in its frame
As you look deep
into the picture
Then tell me
what you see
Because we all
have a hidden story
In the pictures we see
Just waiting to share
With someone
In a thousand
Unspoken words

A Reflection Of Freedom

Freedom begins
With the red
White and Blue
For this
Is a reflection
Of the Red
White in You
We will always
Have to fight
To defend her
And
To keep her free
For this
Is the spirit
That lives
With in me
And
Because of this
You have
Your freedom today
At the price
Of Americans
Who have died
Defending her
And protecting her
So remember
When you see
The colors
Flying high
In the sky
We are
The reflection
Of the Americans
Past and present
Who are proud
To Keep You Free
Even to this day
To the Red
White and Blue
In Honor

And in Pride
Forever
And
Forever Free
For this is a reflection
Of you and me

SPEAK YOUR OWN WORDS

Let one man
Start something
Then
Let another man
Finish it
For this
Will be a story
That we can all read
And share
For it is not
Of his own words
But of my own
So this
Will be something
That we can share
As we read
Our own words

BEHIND THE WALL OF A BARRICADE

For the words I speak
Are unknown to you
And
The words you speak
Are unknown to me
So
The gestures I make
To communicate
Are blind to you
As
The gestures you make
Are blind to me
So
What I hear
You can not hear
And
What you hear
I too
Do not hear
So
What ever we see
It will always be
Something different
Between you and me
Because
Our words
Are scattered
And
Our tongues
Are twisted
As our eyes
Are blind
Behind the wall
Of a barricade

SACRED WORDS

For the spirit
has spoken
And the beat
is out
To all
who will listen
So listen
to the beat
And hear
the words
As the spirit sings
Only to those
who will listen

To Walk In His Shadow

Living a life
Without sin
Is living
In heaven
With him
And
Living a life
In sin
Is living
On earth
With out him
But we can
Live our lives from sin
If we focus on him
For there is
No other way
To live
But to live
Threw him
For he
showed us the way
As his son
Stretched out his arms
And said
I love you
this much
For this
Is just a reminder
Of Gods Love
For you and me

ALONG THE WAY

He doesn't know
If its ok
To go outside
And play

He doesn't even know
His name

So he tries
To use other names
Along the way

Just to say
He belongs to someone

And that he is apart
Of something
Along the way

Writings On The Wall

Any time
any place
I will try
to leave my name
but not in shame
for the words I write
are as free
as I can be.
So go ahead
And read
what you see
But please
Remember
The words I write
Are not in shame
because
they are written
From my heart
And
in my name

SSGT Ralph Lee Butler, Jr.

A Reflection From The Past

For what you see
is me today
But
what you need to see
is the past
of yesterday
For this
is becoming
nothing but a memory
Even
to our four fathers
As they lay
In their graves
Because the pride
and the respect
is fading away
So threw many wars
Torn
Burnt
and even Scared
But still yet
she stands before me
high in the sky
Showing me
The pride
that she has
So in return
I will
protect her
for she
is still free
So can't you see
what she means to me
Because I for one
Will not
Let her become
A fallen memory
Of the past
Because she
Still lives

In the hearts of many
And you can still see
a reflection of her
In my eyes
As she stands
Before you and I

Written by
Ralph L Butler Jr
Rowdy

To Believe In Yourself

You must
Believe in yourself
So others
Will believe in you
As well
So when
We take the first step
Then others
Are sure to fallow
So this
is real simple
To say and do
Because
we need to lead
by example
Then
And only then
Will great leaders
come from this
Only
When we believe
In ourselves

OUR PATH AS THEY CROSS

May the sun shine on you
And
Keep you warm

Let the stars guide you
On threw the night

So
When we meet

We can say

Our paths have meet

Not only
Threw the day
But
Threw the night

Then
We can hear the winds say

Have a good day
And good night

WHY

Why
can we not speak
From our own tongue
Without the fear
Of saying something wrong

Why
Can we not see
From our own eyes
Without the fear
Of seeing something
We should not see

Why
Can we not feel
From our own hearts
Without the fear
Of something
Tearing it apart

Why
Can I not be me
If I live
In the land
of the free
The land
of opportunity

Oh why
Just tell me
Why this might be

Where Does It Rest

For the ribbons
And the medals you see
On my chest
It is a reflection
Of our past
So every time
I see those medals
It reminds me
Of the soldiers
That we lost
Each and ever one
Even thou
You say
it's in honor
To see these ribbons
But I
do not feel that way
Because
all I want to see
Is those soldiers
Back by my side
For that
Is the honor
I want today
When
We all
come back alive
For one life lost
Is one to many
For this
Is an honor
When we all stand
And say
All present
And
Accounted for
Sir
So I ask of you
Is the honor
On my chest
Or
By my side

The Northern Lights

The northern lights
Has a language
Of it's own

Bright
and
full of colors

Colors
Like a rainbow

That comes
From the rains
And
from the mist
Of a waterfall

As the sun light glistens
Threw natures moisture

But only
with sound

As the water falls
From above

But at night
The northern lights
Will speak out
Like city lights

In waves
Like the open seas
Coming
To the shores

Yet
it is in silence

But
It still speaks

To those
Who look
To the northern sky

They
Will see them dance
In many waves

As
The lights shine
and glow
In many colors

For this
Is the northern lights

SOFT SPOKEN

THE WORDS
ARE ONLY AS PURE
AS THE HEART
CAN BE

FOR THE ACTIONS
ARE ONLY AS SOFT
AS THE VOICE
WILL BE

SO
IF YOUR HEART IS PURE
AND
YOUR WORDS ARE SOFT
THEN
YOUR VOICE WILL SPEAK
ONLY
WITH THE WORDS
OF PEACE

When I Write

When I write
I'm like
A different kind of person
Because I go
To a place
Deep within my soul
Where only
The heart can listen
For this
Is only a vision
An image
seen
Only by me
But
to those
who will listen
Will see an image
As if
it was a dream
But only
when I write
So
I'll let my mind wonder
As
I let my heart speak
For these
are the words
I love to speak
To all
Who will listen

A DRIFTING TUMBLEWEED

I'm like a tumbleweed
Out in some fields
Crossing the prairies
Of the great divide
No barbwire fences
Or boundaries
To hold
Or pin me in
For I am free to go
As I may roam
As the winds shall blow
Bright as the sun
And as full as the moon
As I may roam
For I have
No places to be
And no need to hurry
As the winds will carry me
In where I may roam
So the open prairies
Of the great divide
Shall always be
Just my home
That I will always
Have to roam
Like a tumbleweed
Drifting
And tumbling alone

The Cost Of A Soldiers Life

I'm not here
to save the world
I'm here
to try
and save
a soldiers life
And
at this cost
I might loose my own
So if I do
I know
I did my best
Because
they will lay me
with the rest
and I know
They too
tried to do the same
for we are here
To protect each other
And I can say
It is a good day
to die
But today
is not my day
Because I got
My brothers
By my side
But
If something
should fail
Do not
blame them
For we
are in the battle
To try
and save
A soldiers life
For one life lost
Is one to many

SSGT RALPH LEE BUTLER, JR.

So I hope
And prayer
It does not come
at the cost
of a soldiers life

A GOLDEN ROSE

For the rose
I give to you
It is like
A candle light
Shinning
Like the moon at night

For the peddles that fall
Let them be tender
And
Soften your path
As you walk
Threw the night

But let not
The thorns cut you
Or
Bleed your heart

But let my words
And
My voice be felt
Let them
Comfort you

As I give to you
In open arms
A golden rose
That is
MY HEART

WORDS FROM A HEART

I feel
everyone
Has something to share

But Only
If they
Are not scared

To share something
From there hearts

Without the fear
Of being hurt

So
When we share

We never share
Enough
From our hearts

For this
Is a block

That we have built
Around ourselves

Because
This is
Our human nature
Of how
We survive

But if
There was away
To remove this block

Then
And only then

We can open our hearts

Oh what a day
This would be
For you
And me

Without the fear
Or the pain

If Everyone
Could share something
As free
as you want to be

With the words
Only
From your heart

SSGT RALPH LEE BUTLER, JR.

CHANGE A LIFE

CHANGE A LIFE
AND ADD A FRIEND
FOR THE LIFE YOU CHANGE
MIGHT BE
YOUR OWN

An Angel Just For Me

The angel in my life
Is the angel of my life
That has been sent from heaven
So thank you lord
For sending me
Such an angel
That is for me
Because without a dout
I am married to
That angel
That you sent to me
Cause she is always
Looking after me
So thank you lord
Once again
For sending me
Such an angel
That is still
Here with me
An angel
Just for me

Written by
Ralph L Butler Jr
Rowdy

COMING TOGETHER AS ONE

Our eyes are blind
Our ears are def
And our tongues are frozen

Because
We can't come together
As one

So
We need to listen
To our Four Fathers

As there spirit speaks
To you and I

So let our eyes see
What we should see

Let our ears hear
What we should hear

Let our tongues speak
What we should speak

So then
We'll be able to see
what this world
Has really become

As we are able
to hear
what this world
Is trying to say

Then we can speak
And over come
In a group
That is united
As one

The Heart & Mind Of A Child

The heart
of a child

As they mimic
A soldier

For they do not know

What they do
Or
what it means

As they mimic
our salute

But soon
and soon enough

They will remember
what they saw

When they see
another child

That mimics
his salute

Just
as he did
a long time ago

When he
Was a child too

So
from this

It might be
just a mimic
you see

But
What I see

Is still
a salute

not only
from a child

But
from a heart

That is pure
and proud

To mimic
our salute

For this
Is the heart
And the mind
Of a child

THE HIDDEN WORDS
IN THE SILENCE
OF A TEAR

Tears are real words
That are only spoken
From the heart
As they fall

Searching for answers
And understanding
As emotions run high
Deep in heart of the soul
As the tears
Begin to fall

For they are truly
Some of the most powerful
And unspoken words
That many
Will never see
Or ever hear
As they begin to fall

But they still remain
As unspoken words
In the heart of my soul...
As they fall

But yet they bleed
With lonely tears
That only I
Will ever see..

So from the hidden words
That will fall
And from the silence
Of the tears...

Who can fathom
The hidden words
In the silence
Of a tear

Written by
Ralph L Butler Jr
(Rowdy)

BECAUSE OF THE ABUSE

My heart
will bleed for yours
And my tears
will fall for yours as well
And
because of the wounds
that I carry
For they
will not heal
And the scares
will not mend
Because
I know
It will happen
Over
and over again
Until the day
That I am gone
I will be
Laying in a field
Of green pastures
Then
I will be
Surrounded
by many angles
Sheltered
By there wings
And covered
In there love
But still
my heart will bleed
And my tears will fall
For you all
Because the pain
Has not been forgotten
And the scares
Are too deep to mend
All because
of the abuse
to a child

Sharing My Words

I am as good
as I want to be
But yet
I am better
than you think
I might be
So the writings
are the texture
of many words
that are written by me
So as I share these words
the tone of my voice
will carry them
As I share them out loud
For all of you to hear
and to see
how the heart will speak
of what I see
and
for what I feel.
So if you want to write
Put yourself
in my shoes.
Then feel the beat
as your fingertips
start to move
across the path
of a piece of paper.
Or even better yet
a piece of my life
So Feel free
and let the words speak
as you write those words
beneath your feet
For this is the magic
An image of you
As you read
And repeat
I am
as good

as I want to be
But yet
I am better
than you think
I might be

True & Pure Words

TRUE WORDS
WILL COME
FROM THE HEART
IF YOU
LET THE HEART SPEAK

FOR THESE WILL BE
THE PURE WORDS
THAT YOU WILL SEE
AND SPEAK

ONLY
IF AND WHEN
YOU LEARN
TO LET THE HEART SPEAK

MY SPIRIT WILL LIVE

LET MY LIFE
NOT
BE IN VAIN

LET MY NAME
NOT
GO IN SHAME

SO
BLESS THOSE
THAT ARE AROUND ME

THEN
LET MY VOICE
BE HEARD

AS MY WORDS
ARE SPOKEN
FROM DEEP WITHIN

SO
I MAY LIVE
ONCE AGAIN

FOR THIS
IS MY SPIRIT
THAT WILL SPEAK
IN THE WIND

JUST A HEAD STONE AWAY

My daddy loved me
just like he loved you.
If he was here today
he would still
protect me and you.
I sure do miss him
But one day soon
I will be brave
and I will be
just like him
And I too
will protect you
just like he
protected me
and you
and one day soon
I will see him
and that's
when I
can salute him
not only
as soldier
but as his son
as well

A JOURNEY BY REQUEST

With honor
And with pride
We will do
His request...
As we walk
Side by side
The trails
That we've walked together...
So many times before
But now
We shall hike the trails
All once more
To his request
A journey
That will honor him
Because
Of his request
As we carry him
Not only
In our hearts
And in our minds
But in our spirit
as well
And forever
we will
As we travel this journey together
Just one more time...
A journey of honor
So that he may rest
Right here
In the wilderness
Because
That was
His last request
As we lay his ashes
Out to rest

Written by
Ralph L Butler Jr
Rowdy

BY FOOT AND FOOT ALONE

This is what I call
A special mission
Because it is so unique
And quite different
From the rest
But still yet
It is a mission
Because it is to honor
One of our fallen
That is a WWII Vet
But it can not be done
On a bike
Or even from a cage
For this can only be done
By foot and foot alone
As we walk into the wilderness
Of the Sierra Nevada's
Which we'll hike the trails
Of the Pacific Crest
And the John Muir
For these are the trails
That he remembers best
So that we can lay his ashes
All to rest
So that he is free
As the wilderness
That surrounds him
As it takes him away
Ashes to ashes
And dust to dust
I am now free to roam
The mountains
And the valleys
Of the wilderness

Written by
Ralph L Butler Jr
Rowdy

Rowdy-man
The Oklahoma Poet

THE LIFE OF THE MAN...

A Teacher
A Legend
And An Icon
Built All Into One

For this is the man
That was my dad
For a short time

You see
He was my foster dad

But I messed things up
And I had to leave
All because
of my stupidity

But his love for me
never changed
Because he loved me
anyway

But I still
had to move on
And go about my way
All because of the things
That I had done

But then one day
I wanted to see him
So after 20 some years

This
is what he had to say

My prodigal son
Has come home
And I thought
I would never live
to see this day

As my son came home
To me today

As tears
Filled our eyes
As we sat
Side by side
Talking
About the things
From the past

And for the man
That I'm talking about
His name is Ken
Ken Hargreaves
But many
Just call him Harv

But I will always
call him dad

Because
That is
What he is
To me

An icon
That still lives
In me today

But I got some bad news
On this fathers day

That he
is in the hospital
And not
doing well

So at 90
And a WWII Vet
That went to college
At the University of California

Right here in Berkeley
Which would of been
Like Harvard to me
To become a Teacher
To teach mankind
About the history
Of our land

As he gave of himself
To all of those
That surrounded him most

And a true
Boy Scout Leader
That taught us all
All kinds of things

And from a Troop
That I remember
most of all
Troop 1015

For that is where
He gave me hope
And a whole lot more

As he started
to be my dad
Just like that
In a small town
Called Twain Harte

A place we call
Whispering Pines

So you see
He hiked many trails
Throughout the wilderness
Of Sierra Nevada's
Just a piece of history
Throughout the years

Discovering
Who we can be
As his spirit lives
In the history
of the wilderness
That he
will always see

He loved to fish
As he and I
Once did

So all I can do
Is to hope and pray
That someday
I can be
Just like him
Not only
a fisherman
But a fisher of men
Don't you see

As he gave of himself
To those
that needed him most

As he told me
To look to the trees
And you will see
How they lean
As they reach out
For something
Like you and me

For this is called
Heliotropism
Reaching for the light

Just like
I have alway done
By reaching
And reaching out

For something
I did not see

For within the words
That are written above
They have a lesson
That can be learned
As they have been told
To you and I
By a true leader
A leader of men

So thank you dad
for a lesson well learned
That we can still
learn today
Thats all from you
As history is written
From you and I

For this
is the life
Of a great man

A Teacher
A Legend
And An Icon
Built All Into One

Written by your son
(Little Harv)
Ralph L Butler Jr

Dedicated to
Barbara Hargreaves
(Barb) my mom

In loving memory of
Ken Hargreaves
(Harv) my dad
Oct. 3rd, 1921 -
June 23rd, 2012

THE TOAST OF A LIFETIME

I left this earth today
But I leave you with
the knowledge
Of that
In which I taught
Not only to you
But to all
That heard my words
So I leave with you
The wisdom
Of 90 years
of my life
So here's to you
My family
And my friends
That have been
A part of my life
Celebrate my life
And celebrate the journey
That I have traveled
From the mountains
To the valleys
To the meadows
Of the wilderness
In which I still live
May my words now be
Like the smell of the pine trees
That you breathe
And let us all
Be as free
As the rivers and streams
As they flow together
Like you and me
Because this is now
Where I will be
In the wilderness
Where I am free
With the trees
And the streams
Of the wilderness

That you see
Harv
Oct 3rd 1921
June 23rd 2012

Written by
Ralph L Butler Jr

LIVE FOR THE JOURNEY
AND NOT
FOR THE RESULTS
AND THE BENEFITS
OF THE JOURNEY
FOR THEN
YOU WILL KNOW
THAT YOU
HAVE LIVED A LIFE
WITHIN A JOURNEY
TO THAT WHICH IS
A JOURNEY OF LIFE
FOR THERE IS
NO BEGINNING
AND THERE IS
NO END
BECAUSE
IT'S JUST THAT
A JOURNEY
A JOURNEY
WITH NO END....
AND A JOURNEY
TO NO END....
BECAUSE LIFE ITSELF
IS THAT
OF A JOURNEY

Written by
Ralph L Butler Jr
Rowdy

TWO DIFFERENT SIDES

If you
show me heads
Then I
will show you tails

But
If you
show me tails
Then I
will show you heads

So just remember
There will always be
Two sides to a coin

So it is said

And now
show me
A person
that is strong
Then I
will show you
That,
that person
is week

And now
show me
A person
that is week
Then I
will show you
That,
that person
is strong

So no matter
How we see it
There will be
Two different sides
To everyone

Because Of A Dream

Because of a dream
I can not see
what is going on
around me
but a reflection
will always be seen
by those
that are around me
for they
are be able to see
what I can not see
and they
are be able to feel
what I can not feel
even thou
I can not see
the reflection
of myself
but those that are close
might get hurt
without ever knowing
that I have hurt you at all
even thou
I had good intentions
something
someway or another
will over come me
all because
I saw something
from my pass
just like a reflection
or even a dream
a dream
that I still carry
deep within myself
or even
some kind of hope
that just
maybe.....
or someday.....
as it seems to block out everything

that is around me
so because of the hurt
that is still inside me
even thou
it is something from my pass
some things
that has not changed
like being left behind
or just being left out.
Even thou
I'm still hanging on, …
I got to stop
and let go
then
I'll take a look around
and when I see you there
I hope
that I can realize
that it is you
that I'm hurting
as well as myself
so because
you are still
hanging on
I got to stop
and let go
of this foolish dream
for it
will never happen
and just remain
nothing but a dream
so before it is to late
I will turn to you
then
and only then
can I start living
a new dream
because you are
the dream
I need to be living in
and the dream
I need to dream

Leadership

If you lead
with your heart
Then many
will fallow

But
if you lead
Because of your greed
Then many will fall
With no leadership
At all

So
Put all things aside
And remember
Who you are

Because
Good leaders
Will lead
From there hearts
Or not at all

So show no favors
And be fair to all
If you want to be
A leader
With leadership
To all

HE PROMISED ME

My arms
will always be
around you
when you need me

For I
will always
carry you
in a time of need

And I
will always be
by your side
when you look
for me

For this
is a promise
that I will keep
even
after the death of me

Because
I am the light
in the path
so you can see

For I am the life
that surrounds you
in every way

And still today
I will
hold out my arms
and say

I LOVE YOU THIS MUCH

with every breath
that I take

For this
is the promise
that I made

LIFE WITHIN IT'S SELF

LIFE IS AN OPPORTUNITY
And they say
it only comes
once in a life time
SO WE MUST BENEFIT FROM IT.

LIFE IS A GAME
That we have played
and played all to well
some will be winners
and some will be losers
but remember
for this is a game
that will be remembered
SO PLAY THE GAME
AND PLAY IT WELL

LIFE IS A DREAM
That only you can dream
so live your dream
and live it well
but you still got to remember
that only you
can make it come true
SO SOME DAY
YOU JUST MIGHT REALIZE IT.

LIFE IS A CHALLENGE
That you will have to decide
witch way to go
and what direction
you will travel
SO GO AHEAD AND MEET IT
HEAD ON

LIFE IS A DUTY
That you will have to perform
so go ahead and finish what you set
out to do
AS YOU COMPLETE IT.

LIFE IS BEAUTY
So every thing you see
there will be something special
that you will remember
for days to come
SO AHEAD AND ADMIRE IT.

LIFE IS A PROMISE
That will give us hope
even when it is broken
so we must believe in something
even if we are not sure
of what we see
or even what we feel
BUT SOMETHING WILL FULFILL
IT.

LIFE IS SORROW
That will make you fall
but you will stand once again
stronger than before
ONLY
WHEN YOU OVERCOME IT.

LIFE IS A SONG
That will beat
in your mind
and in your heart
as you walk along
your own path
SO SING IT
AND SING IT OUT LOUD

LIFE IS A STRUGGLE
That shows us
that we will have to fight
each and ever day
day in and day out
SO WE MUST ACCEPT IT
FOR THERE IS NO OTHER WAY

LIFE IS A TRAGEDY
that will knock
at our front door
and it might
just knock you down
SO WE WILL HAVE TO
CONFRONT IT
WHEN THAT DAY COMES

LIFE IS LUCKY
So go ahead
and wish upon a star
for the wish you make
it might be more
than you bargained for
SO GO AHEAD
AND WISH IT

LIFE IS AN ADVENTURE
That only you will travel
each an every day of your life
may you see something new
as you travel on your path
but there's going to be a challenge that
you will have to take
SO GO AHEAD
AND TAKE THAT DARE

FOR LIFE
IS JUST LIFE
So we will live it
to it's fullest
ONLY
IF WE ARE WILLING
TO LIVE IT

SO THIS IS LIFE
AND LIFE
WITHIN IT'S SELF

The Night Of Christmas Eve

It was the night before Christmas,
and all threw the fields
Some soldiers were watching
out over a view
There weapons were ready
And ready at will
But Only In danger
If danger appeared
For this was an action
That would keep us safe
As the others were resting
so close and near

As I stood watch
on this Christmas eve
I started thinking of home
with the memories I had
Like mamma in the kitchen
cooking something up fine
with the smell of fresh cider
that sat beside her
For this was the memories
that went threw my mine
Even thou I'm standing here
With this old tin cup
I will drink this battlefield brew
that was made of muck

Then out in the distance
there they came
The enemy that I had fought
ready To make there name
As our soldiers jump up
And out of their racks
we where locked and loaded
just like that
Ready and willing
to defend each other
in just a flash

Then it all unfolded
Before our eyes
For they are coming
But only in peace
Holding a flag
that was all white
My eyes were lost
With such a sight
So cheers rung out
From Deep inside
But I never let go
of the fear inside
for they had no weapons
Of any kind
As there eyes teared up
and began to fall
I knew right then
this war was over
and we would soon go home.

For the news had spread
Like fire flies
But we still stood guard
just in case
We were hoping
that this was true
and not
some kind of prank
or surprise
For some of us whistled,
and others
shouted out loud.
It's over
And we get to go home
thank you lord
for keeping us safe
For it's all over
And now we can go home

Then tears began to fall
as we all gathered round
And then,

it was confirmed
it is all over
and we are going home

Right then and there
the memories started to flash
all around in my head
as I took a look back
and as I was stood there
letting it soak on in
Then I saw my brothers
and sisters
coming together
at the end
then someone said out loud
some day
we will
see each other again
so until that day
may your travels be safe because
we will
always have your 6
For we
are your family here today
on this Christmas Eve
So we hugged
and shook each others hands
As we said our goodbyes
But then I heard
someone say
As we parted or ways
"Merry Christmas to all,
and to all
a good-night!"

D.O.D

What is D.O.D.?
It is what I call:
Dysfunctional Observational
Disorder.
That is D.O.D.
So next time,
someone says,
they saw you
doing something
that you should not
have been doing.
Then tell them:
they got D.O.D.
Or when you caught
with your hand
in the cookie jar,
then tell them:
they got D.O.D.
So any time
you need a way out of something,
just tell them:
they got D.O.D.
PS.
Your Welcome
and that's my story
and I'm sticking to it.

OPEN WOUNDS

It has been said
that time
will heal all wounds
but I do not agree
because the wounds
are still alive
so as time goes on
the mind will try
to cover them up
that is why
we carry the scars
that do remain
so now the pain
is not as strong
as it use to be
but it does remain
so the wounds
and the scars
are still in bedded
deep inside
for they
are never gone

An Abused Child

For this is a true story:
More than you will ever know.

A poor little child,
Once said to his mother:
"Mommy,
I just painted the sheets
with the lipstick"
and the mother broke out
in such an outraged.
Hitting the child,
repeatedly,
until the child
was knocked unconscious.
Then she tried to apologized,
for what she had done.
But it was to late.
The child's little heart
had stopped beating.
and the bedroom sheets read:
"Mom I love you"

Try and share this one
so the voice of an abused child,
can be heard.

Then let us all come together
and try to stop this abuse.
For it is our voices
and our actions,
that can help a child,
before it is to late.
Remember;
This happens every day,
and I know this to well.
Because I too
was an abused child
and the scares
are deeper
than you will ever know,

and the wounds
can not heal
and the scares
can not mend,
because it is in-bedded
deep within.
So it is very sad to see
what is hidden
behind the walls
that you can not see

THIS IS OUR OATH

Operation Brother Tight
Rio Bravo
Delta Force
Bravo Company
Echo 6th to the 12th Cav

"This Is Our Oath"

There is no mercy
For the weak
So the strong
Will show no weakness
Because of the fight we take
There will be no mistake
But if you apologize
For what you have done
Then that in its self
Is a sign of weakness
For this is the honor
And the pride
That only comes from inside
Not only by me
But for my team as well

THE BECOMING OF ONE

When you fight
You will fight as a team
When you fight as a team
you will fight as one
So your mind will think
as you react to the situation
So for every situation
There is only one solution
So never second guess yourself
or your judgment
just react to the situation
and everyone will fallow
When you are a team
standing as one

SSGT RALPH LEE BUTLER, JR.

JUST A CALL OF DUTY

Someone behind a desk
once said
lets take names
and kick some ass

But a soldier said:
Lets kick ass,
then you
can take the names
Because
we still got work to do

So now
that we
have eliminated the treat
you can come out
from under your desk
and write the names
as you wish

For the task
you put before me
might be tough
But the will
behind me
Will always
be stronger
than your task

Walk Soft And Tread Easy

Walk soft
and tread easy
For you
are a reflection
from your own words
So let the words flow
in honor
and in peace
For this is an action
that cones from within
So take a stand
And let your pride shine
oh let it shine
from within
because you are
a reflection
from your own words

THE COST OF FREEDOM

Freedom is not free
For it comes at a price
The price of a father
or even a son
For that was back then
But
if you stop
And take a look around
You will see
That the price will come
From Mothers
and daughters as well
Because
this is the price
Of our freedom today
And all
will be recognized
For they
Are not forgotten

If he spoke to you today
He would simple say
The fight is not over....
For it has just begun....
For that's
The kind of man
A teacher
That my Foster Dad was
For he
is just one
of the reasons
That I have survived
As I carry his words
And his wisdom
for all of us
to read
and to share
here today

Ken Hargreaves
Oct. 3, 1921
June 23, 2012

DIRECTION

He gives us direction
But the choices we make
Sometimes makes obstacles
In the directions we travel
But threw him
All things are possible
If we let the lord
Lead the way

A TRAVELERS CROSS

North and south
East and west
For I am your compass
That gives you light
and direction
So no matter
Where you are
And no mater
Where I am
Our roads
Will always cross
Even
In a time of prayer
As you travel
With the travelers cross
So remember
I will always be
Right their
When ever you need me
From that cross

The Travelers Cross

A LETTER FROM THE BOX

At one time
In my courier
We had
What we called
A drop box
That hung on the wall
Which would hold
Our letters
And our dog tags
Aw well
As it came to be
But if
We never came back
A mark was made
In our honor
In remembrance
Of those
That had fallen
And someone
From among our ranks
Would take
Their letter home…
And for I myself
Had only lost
That of one
And still
That is one to many
From among our ranks
As I took
His letter home
That read:

For you and I
Have no home
For we grew up
In foster homes…
So my home
And my family
Is here with you…
So take care

My brother
Take care
My friend
As you read
My letter…
And remember this
For I will always
Have you six…

And that indeed
He did
But now the thing
That hurts me most
As I remember
My brother…
For I have lost
His letter
And his dog tags
As well
In the Mannford fire
That took it all
But my memories still live
As I remember
My brother
And those
That we call
Our friends
For we are still a family
Among ourselves
Even
To the end…

Written by
SSGT Ralph L Butler Jr
Rowdy

A SOLDIERS STORY
FROM THAT
OF THE PAST

MY HEART BLEEDS
NOT ONLY TODAY
BUT EVERY DAY
AS I REMEMBER THOSE
LIKE YESTERDAY
AS THE STORY GOES
ALL GAVE SOME
AND SOME GAVE ALL
AND FOR THIS
THEY ARE NOT FORGOTTEN
AS TEARS STILL FALL
FROM THAT OF MY OWN EYES
FOR THEY HAVE BEEN HIDDEN
DEEP IN MY HEART
AND IN MY SOUL
FOR A VERY LONG TIME
AND SOME STILL REMAIN
IN THE HEARTS
AND THE SOULS
OF OUR KIND
SO NEED I SAY MORE
AS I STAND HERE
BUT NOT ALONE
WITH A GHOST
FROM THE PAST
IN SPIRIT
AND IN SOUL
AS IF I TOO
WAS A GHOST
LIKE A SOLDIER
FROM THE PAST
THAT IS STANDING HERE
WITH ME
AS WE HONOR
AND REMEMBER
THOSE VETS
FOR WE ARE STILL
A BAND OF BROTHERS

TO THE END
THAT ARE NOT FORGOTTEN
AND WE ARE UNITED
INTO A UNITY
OF JUST ONE
THAT I FOR ONE
WILL REMEMBER
FOR YEARS TO COME
FOR THAT IS JUST PART
OF OUR HONOR
THAT COMES FROM DEEP
WITHIN
LIKE AN UNSPOKEN OATH
AN OATH
THAT WE'LL LIVE BY
AND AN OATH
THAT WE'LL DIE BY
ALL BECAUSE
WE ARE BROTHERS
TO THE END
AND FOR THE WORDS
THAT SAYS
SEMPER FI
MIGHT SAY IT BEST...
AS WE ALL
COME TO REST
SO SEMPER FI
AND
GOD BLESS...
FOR THESE
ARE JUST SOME WORDS
THAT ARE WRITTEN
FROM OUR PAST
THAT REMAIN
IN OUR HEARTS
AND IN OUR MINDS
FOREVER
THAT YOU MIGHT
BE ABLE TO SEE
AS YOU READ
A PIECE OF HISTORY
FROM A SOLDIERS STORY

JUST
LIKE THIS...
SO DONT LET IT SLIP AWAY
FROM THAT
OF YOUR FINGER TIPS
AS OUR MEMORIES LIVE
IN A SOLDIERS STORY
JUST LIKE THIS
THAT STILL REMAINS
A PART OF THE PAST...

Written by
SSGT Ralph L Butler Jr
Rowdy

MY LITTLE GRANDMA

There is a day
That I remember
Even thou
It was
so long ago
But yet
I can still
see it today.
Like Grandma
And Little Grandma,
Cooking tamales up
In the kitchen
Way back
in the day
For Little Grandma
Has been gone
for some time now
So now this honor
I pass onto you
For you
are my Little Grandma now
And you told me
Not to long ago
I remember you
You are Ralphie
And
I remember when
your mother
Kept hitting you
with a shoe
So I hit her back.
A lady like this
Stood with a fist
Protecting me
So I too
will stand with her
Because she is
My Little Grandma
For she
might be small

and frail
But yet
Her memories
Where strong
As she remembered me
Even though
She has now
passed on
I will say once more
to you again
Thank You
Thank You for standing up
for me
For you
will always be
My Little Grandma
That protected me
Love your grandson:
Ralphie

SHE STILL LIVES

She still lives
but not
in her own body
but in the lives
of her children
and her grand children
as well
so what you see
will be her spirit
that lives
in her children
and her grandchildren
as well
and because of this
she still lives
in all of you

Only God
Knows what is best
So judge no one
But yourself
As you pass
Your judgment
Upon yourself
And as you walk
In your path
You shall find
A reflection
Of your past
All from something
That you seek
That comes
From your past...

TAKE THE WHEEL

In your troubles
And in your sorrows
In your disasters
And in your fears
Let Jesus
Take the wheel
For he is the pilot
That will guide you
Through the trials
And the tribulation
If you would only
Let him
Take the wheel
For he
Is always there
When ever
You need him
So trust him
And call
Upon his name
And let him
Guide you
As he
Takes the wheel....

Written by
Ralph L Butler Jr
Rowdy

A Moment of Memory

If you see something
that takes your breath away
Cherish that moment forever
Because in a blink of an eye
It has already changed
And it will never
be of the same...
For it is already gone...

RESTORING YOURSELF

There was a time
That I remember
When I was young

When we all
did things together

Like a family
would have done

But then
it was taken away

For one reason
or another

So things were lost
And The Holidays
where gone

for everything
was gone
just like that

It was like
it might of never been

But
it was still
in my mind
and in my heart

So the things
from the past
I went ahead
and blocked them out

so that
I would not get hurt

and then
I acted like a fool

As if
I didn't want to believe
or even see
the things from the past

But
as time goes on
and we grow old

something
that we see
will trigger our memories
from the past

that's
when we can start
restoring the belief
In the things
that are in our minds
and in our hearts

AN OPEN WOUND

when the heart bleeds
so does the words
but still yet
the heart will keep beating
as the words go silent
because no one
wants to see or hear
what is going on around them
So then
the words are dead
until the heart has mended
then
the words shall live
once again
as they are spoken
for time
can only heal
what is broken
but still
the scare remain
that go unspoken

OPEN FEELINGS RUN TRUE

I hope the tears
are falling in peace
with love and joy

But let it not
fall in sorrow
or in pain

Because
no matter how they fall
I'll feel the effects
in witch they fall

For this is the feelings
that run from the tears
as they fall

THE WORDS WE SHARE

For the words we share
Are in laughter
And in sorrow
But they are
the words we share
When we all come together

LIVING IN LOVE

The day
That I stop loving you
Is the day
That I close my eyes
Forever

So then
That will be the day
That I
Take my last breath

But until that day
The love I have for you
You will always see
As I breath the air
That surrounds
You and me

For this
Is the living love
That lives
And breaths
Within me

THE SPIRIT
OF MOTHER EARTH

For the mountains
Are the peeks
That let's us see
Out over the valleys
Of our homes

For the streams
Are the paths
To our rivers
That will lead us
To the great lake
That we all call
An ocean
A great body of water
That will flow
To the ends of the world

For the sun is the light
That let's us see
Threw the day
And at night
The moon shall give us light
For its just a reflection
From the sun
So we can still see
Threw out the night

For this
Is our Mother Earth
That she has given unto us
In an open
And free spirit
That we shall cherish
And hold sacred
For the rest of our lives

So now
That we can see the things

That she has given to us all
Let your spirit free
And let it see the things
That are around you

For this is not a dream
Or a vision of any kind
For these are the things
That you will see today

So is there anything
That we need to change
Or is it still the same

If it is not the same
What is it
That we have changed
So then
What is it
That we need to change
To keep her spirit free

So let us fix
Whatever we have destroyed
Or even damaged
So we can give back
To Mother Earth
What is hers

So then her spirit
Will live
Once again

THE REALM OF YOUR SLEEP

For it has been said
when you
close your eyes
that your mind
really goes to work
thinking about the things
that not only
happen today
but from years
of our past
so then
when you open them up
all the things
from our past
will flash
before our eyes
but yet
it still remains
in our memories
and in our minds
so go ahead
and close your eyes
so you may rest
in the realm
of your dreams

A FREE SPIRIT

YOU CAN SAY
THAT WHEN
OUR INNER SPIRIT
IS SET FREE
THAT WE
CAN SEE THE THINGS
THAT LIFE
HAS TO BRING
BUT ONLY
WHEN WE
ARE TRULY FREE

A FRIEND

A FRIEND
IS THE BEST THING
THAT YOU CAN EVER HAVE
AND AT THE SAME TOKEN
IT IS THE BEST THING
THAT YOU CAN EVER BE

WHAT WE DO

What We Do
For Ourselves
Will Only Die
But
What We Do
For Others
Will Always Live

MY SHADOW

For I am my own best friend
Nor will I ever fight with you
Or even complain
about the things that you do
as you follow me around
Even as you mimic me
everywhere I go
For I do not owe you anything
Nor do you owe me
But I still
owe it all to myself
So we will survive
even in the hardest of times
So remember
when we see each other
I am your best friend
For these are the words
that are spoken and shared
from deep within
For we
are each others strength
as we see our spirit move
in a perfect silhouette
from the peaks
of the mountains
to the valleys below us
our voices will be heard
But yet
they are only seen and felt
by each other
across this great land

STEPPING OUTSIDE OF YOUR COMFORT ZONE

A challenge
Is not a challenge
Not until
you step outside
of your comfort zone
Then it becomes a challenge
For this is a new beginning
as a new life begins
when you start living
above and beyond
your own comfort zone

SACRED HONOR

Honor what is sacred
and that which is sacred
shall honor you

For that which is sacred
will come from within
same as the honor
that lives within

So honor
what is sacred

A TRUE COMPANION

FOR WE
WILL NEVER BE ALONE
FOR THEY
ARE ALWAYS BY MY SIDE
AND WE
WILL ALWAYS
HAVE EACH OTHER
NO MATTER WHERE I GO
BECAUSE
IT WILL ALWAYS BE
ME
MYSELF
AND I

TO OVER COME

To win your own battle
You must conquer your fears

TO BE A WINNER

To be a winner
You must be able
to feel the defeat
Then you will see
that everyone
is still a winner

SOLID GROUND

What has happened
In our past
Shall be the foundation
On which we stand
But it is still the wisdom
Of our future
That is at hand

BUILDING YOUR STRENGTH

A Lack of Confidence
Is Just A Sign Of Weakness

For we never have time
to do things right
But
We always have time
to do them over
For this
It is a lack of confidence
looking
for some kind
of an approval
from others
For this
is our human nature
As we start to step forward
So is it really
a lack of confidence
or just a sign of weakness
Whatever it is
It is thriving
on the strength of others

YOUR REACTION

Doubt not
what you think
or even
what you say
For the first thing
that comes to mind
it is more than likely
to be the correct thing
to say
or even do

TO TELL A STORY

I love it
when a picture
tells a story
of a thousand words
That comes
From your own words
but
I love it more
when your heart
tells the story
with a million more

SINGING HEARTS

I CAN HEAR
THE HEARTS SING

AS THEY SING
IN HARMONY

ALL BECAUSE
OF THEIR FRIENDSHIP

THAT THEY HAVE BUILT
THROUGHOUT THE YEARS

FOR THEY
ARE SINGING OUT LOUND
AND SINGING TOGETHER

SO
WHEN YOU HEAR THEM

THEY WILL SING
IN PERFECT HARMONY

FOR THIS
IS THEIR SONG

THAT THEY WILL REMEMBER
FOR YEARS TO COME

SO GO AHEAD
AND LISTEN

BECAUSE
THEIR HEARTS ARE SINING

NOT ONLY TODAY
BUT EVERY DAY
IF YOU ONLY LISTEN

Written by:
Rowdy l butler

LIVING YOUR DREAM TODAY

If we do the things today
That need to be done

Then the things for tomorrow
Will never get done

Because tomorrow
will never come

So go ahead
and do the things
that you wanted to do today

For then I know
with out a doubt

That you are living
your life today

So go ahead
and live your dream

Live that dream
Today

For there is
no tomorrow

UNKNOWN TIME

It can be the day before
or it can be the day after

It can be last year
or it can be this year

No matter what time it is
it will always be
before, during, or after

For it is never too late
and it is never to early

For the future holds the key
to our past

So tell me
is today today
or is today tomorrow
but yet
tomorrow can be today
and today can be yesterday

So is this our past
or is it our future
Because the present
has already passed
or has it

A BLANKET OF COMFORT

May the words
be as soft
and as gentle
As the voices
In the wind
and may it be
as soft
as the roses
that surround you
And may we understand
What we see
And what we feel
As they comfort you
in where you lay...

THE SOLES OF YOUR FEET

For the shoes
That we wear

Tells a story
About the path
That we walk

And within those shoes
Is the character
in which we stand

So remember
Shoes will talk
Even
When we don't

THE OLD
GRANDFATHER CLOCK

It was
some time back
without me ever knowing
that the small hand
on the clock
had moved on up
an hour or two

For It took me by surprise
and little did I know
that I could loose
a piece of time
To history
just like that

For that which I had lost
is only but of time
but it is still lost
and gone forever
for we will never
get it back

All because I did not see
the time that had passed
right before my eyes

So it is
Just that
for we can not
stop the hands
on a clock
from going around
and around
and we can not
go back in time
because
it is already gone
and lost
just like that

as it goes
tick-tock
tick-tock
the hands will keep moving
on this old clock
for it is passing time
just like that
tick-tock
tick-tock
can you hear
the old grandfather clock
tick-tock
tick-tock
as he passes time
just like that

THE WALLACE'S OF IRELAND

May the words
Be as pure
As the heart
As it beats
Like the drums

And the blades
Of your swords
Be as sharp
As your tongues

So as we gather as Knights
Like Knights shall do
In shinning armor
At the realms of our table
And someone say

For I am of the clan
Of the Wallace's
Of Ireland

Then we shall cheer
With the words
That are so divine
As we bring out
The gold-n-me steins

For we are blessed
From the words
That are so divine
For it has been written
On the scrolls of our hearts
And to our brotherhood
That is so divine

So cheers my-Lad
For the freedom at hand
Is worth fighting for
And it is so divine

As we all gather
As Knights

So
From the blood of our hands
To the hearts of Ireland
We are the last
Of our Clan

Rowdy Lee Wallace

CHANGE

We can never
Change the things
That are behind us

But we can
Change the things
That are ahead of us

For that
Which is happening now
Is really to late to change

So what we really
Need to change
Is just ahead of us

Because that
Is never to late to change

WOUNDS FROM THE PAST

No tears
From the pain
Shall fall today
Because the wounds
That we carry
Bleeds no more
Because they themselves
Have no blood
To bleed
For they
Have turned to scars
That holds the pain
And the tears
Deep inside
The souls
And the hearts
Of those
That have been torn
For that is something
That you yourself
Shall never know
Or ever see
As we try
To deal with them
Each and every day
Of our life's
Because this
In its self
Is a struggle
That we live with
From day to day
Each and every day
From the pain
And the memories
Of yesterday
So each
And every day
Of our life's
From here on out
Shall show

No tears
From the pain
and the memories
Of the past
Except for those
That might
Just over flow
But only
When we are alone
As we remember
The wounds
And the memories
From the past

Written by
Ralph L Butler Jr
Rowdy

POST BLOCK & DELETE
WHAT WILL IT BE
FOR A COMPUTER
HAS NO FEELINGS
BUT THE PERSON
ON THE OTHER ENDS DOES
SO REMEMBER THIS
AS YOU POST THOSE WORDS
THAT MANY WILL SEE...
BECAUSE
WE ALL HAVE FEELINGS
AND OPINIONS
IN THE WORDS
THAT WE READ
SO TELL ME
WHAT SHALL IT BE
POST BLOCK AND OR DELETE
BECAUSE
MY CHOICE MIGHT BE
LIKE
COMMENT
OR EVEN SHARE
FROM A POST
THAT I READ
OR EVEN SEE
SO TELL ME NOW
WHAT
SHALL IT BE
AS I COPY
AND PASTE
SOMETHING LIKE THIS...
THAT I SEE...

JUST DO IT TODAY

Just go ahead
And do it today
For there is no other time
Than the time you have today
To do the things
That you wish
You would have of done
yesterday
so
before it is to late
go ahead
and do it today
Because
If you put it off
Until tomorrow
It might just be
to late
So then
You might regret it
For the rest of your life
So remember
That you can not
Turn back the time
And for the time
There is no better time
Than the time of today
So go ahead
And do it today

A SUNSET TO MEMORIES

I'm having a hard time today
For its not like
Any other day
You see
We lost a love one
Early one morning
But yet
When I look around
I can see
That she still lives
In our hearts
And in our minds
So go ahead
And hear these words
Because she lives
In all the words we say
But still yet
Im having a hard day
As I wipe the tears
From my eyes
So I can see
And read
Those loving words
That are so kind
As the sun sets
In the memories
Of our hearts
And in our minds

A TIME TO STAND

There is a moment
In your life
That you will stand
Above and beyond
Any other day

For this is the time
That you will shine
And become
Who you really are

With little
To no warning at all

But still yet
You will survive
And become
One in a million

For no one
Owes you any thing
But still yet
You owe it to yourself
To survive

So
In the split
Of a second
You can make a change
To over come
And adapt

For this is who you are
In just a blink of an eye

So
It does not matter
About the things
From our past

But what does matter
Is the things
That are to come
For they
Are now at hand

Because
It will always be
About the choices
That we make

So remember
That you and only you
Can chose between
Whats right and wrong

For this
Will make you
Who you really are

So feel free
And stand true
To yourself

Because this
Is who you are
And no one else
Can ever be
Like you and me

Written by
SSGT Ralph L Butler Jr
Rowdy

THE UNKNOWN TO FATHOM

You can not fathom
The words of a writer

But you can
Draw a picture
To your own conclusion

So that
You may honor
The words
That have been written

For then
You might understand
What has been written

But then again
Can you fathom
The words
That are written

Because on one
Can really understand
What has been written

But the writer
Himself

Written by
Ralph L Butler Jr
Rowdy

STUCK ON MY MIND

Every time
I hear your name
It just drives me all insane
Every time
Oh every time
I hear your name

And every time
I hear your name
I just stop
And turn around
Just to see
If you are there
Every time
Oh every time
I hear your name

So
I just want to
Turn back time
Just to see you there
For one last time

Because
Every time
I hear your name
It just drives me
All insane
Because
You are stuck
In my mind
And in my heart
Forever
And
Forever more

LOVE WILL SHINE

Love is soft
And kind
With understanding

But hate
Is hard
And meaningless
With no
Understanding

But love will shine
And overcome
With forgiveness

While hate will hide
In the darkness
Of the shadows

But love
Brightens the heart
With peace and joy

While hate
Darkens the heart
And the souls
Of man kind

But it is said
If you live in the light
Then the light
Will live in you
And the shadows
Of the dark
Shall be no more

Because
The warmth of the light
Will bring to life
A new meaning
To the love

SSGT RALPH LEE BUTLER, JR.

That is hidden
Deep within yourself

For this is the life
That I want to live
With peace and joy
From within

Because
Love is soft
And kind
With understanding
But still yet
We can not fathom
What GOD has done

For he is the light
And the way
To the love
That will come
From deep within

A GIFT ONLY FROM GOD

Some times
Gods little gifts
Will come
From a child
And that child
Will touch our hearts
In so many ways
And it is a miracle
A gift
That will only
Come from God

A BAND OF BROTHERS

We are
One nation
Of many brothers

For you know not
What you say
Or even do
When you talk
About the race
Of one another
Because
We all bleed
Like the same
So ask me not
Of my brothers
But ask me
Of my team
For we
Are a unit
Of many brothers
That are
Of the same
For we
Are ready
To shed our blood
Just to protect
One another
For we
Are proud to say
These two words
That are one
Semper Fi
Because
We are
A band of brothers
To Semeper Fidelis
A name
That we live by
And a name
That we

Will die by
Because this
Is our honor
To one another
Which is
a band
Of many brothers
As we all say
Semper Fi

SSGT RALPH LEE BUTLER, JR.

SOMETIMES

Sometimes
The right thing to do
Is to do nothing at all
And let nature itself
Take its course
But it still seems
That the problem
Still remains
That of the same
As we try
To figure it out
And once again
We'll ask ourselves
Time and time again
What is
The right thing....
As we fight a battle
Within ourselves
Trying
To figure it all out
As we say once more
What is
The right thing...
Because only time
Will ever tell...

Maybe
Just maybe
One day
You can take
The hate
Out of your heart
And see the love
From the words
That are written
From the heart
Of another

TEARS IN AN ESCORT
FROM A KIA

Tears filled my eyes
With sorrow
And with pain
As memories flashed
before my eyes
As we escorted
One of our fallen home today
But pride
and honor
Really
Came alive
As I wiped the tears
From my eyes
As I saw Americans
Standing there
Holding flags
And standing tall
With their hands over there hearts
and some
Where even saluting
As we went on by
All from an escort
For one of our fallen
That was a KIA
The number of people
I could not say
But everywhere
I seemed to look
They where there
Paying there respects
And still
I had to wiped away the tears
From my eyes
As I drove on by
It gave me pride
Just to see
How some strangers
Came to be
They parked their cars

Out on the highway
as they saluted
As we went on by
AMERICA
It is still nice to see
The love you have
For your counrty
And your freedom today
So thank you
From a vet
For showing your respect
That many
Will never see
Thank you again
America
Thank you
Oklahoma
And thank you
Shawnee
For showing your respect
To one of our fallen
That is a KIA

Written by:
SSGT Ralph L Butler Jr
Security Specialist
USAF
811X0

IT WILL NEVER BE THE SAME

For what we have seen once
We will never see again
So remember to cherish
What you have seen

For you will only
See it once
For it
Has already changed
In just
A blink
Of an eye

TO WHAT WE SEE

To that
Of what I see
And to that
Of what
I do not see
But may it be
To something
That we both
Shall see
So then
It will be
To that
Of what we see

NOT FORGOTTEN

A nation that forgets
Its defenders
Will itself
Be forgotten
So let us not
Be forgotten
As we all stand
To honor
And remember
One another
In good times
And in sad
For we
Are the defenders
That stands here
Not only today
But every day
With respect
Like we
Have always done
With the colors
Flying proud
And standing tall
All to remember
Its defenders
Of this great nation
So that
We are not forgotten

THE ENTER STRENGTH FROM WITHIN

In the moment
You start to think
About giving up

Is the moment
You need to stop
And think about
The reason why
You hung on
For so long

Then
You will find
A reason
To hang on
A little more

For this
Is what
We will learn
As we overcome
The obstacles
That are in
Our lives

All because
We are stronger
Than before

THE PRIDE OF MY VEST

FOR THIS IS THE PRIDE
THAT RIDES
ON OUR LEATHER

OUR PATCHES
AND OUR PINS
SHOW A CHARACTER
IN WHERE
WE HAVE BEEN

EVEN THOU
THE HONOR
AND THE PRIDE
SHALL ALWAYS LIVE
DEEP INSIDE
THE SOULS
OF OUR KIND

BUT STILL TODAY
SOME
WILL NEVER BE SEEN
OR EVEN WORN
ON THE CHARACTER
OF THAT
IN WHICH YOU SEE

FOR THIS
IS THE UNSPOKEN
THAT YOU
WILL NEVER HEAR
OR EVER SEE

BUT IT STILL REMAINS
IN OUR HEARTS
AND IN OUR MINDS
FOREVER
THAT ONLY WE
SHALL EVER SEE

BUT SOME
JUST MIGHT BE SEEN
ON THE LEATHER
THAT YOU HAVE READ
OR EVEN SEEN

FOR THIS
IS THE CHARACTER
THAT IS IN THE LEATHER
THAT YOU
SHALL REALLY SEE

AND
IT WILL ALWAYS BE
OUR HONOR
AND OUR PRIDE
THAT YOU
SHALL EVER SEE

SO REMEMBER THIS
AS ONE WOULD SAY

THIS IS THE PRIDE
THAT RIDES
ON OUR LEATHER
NOT ONLY TODAY
BUT EVERY DAY

SEMPER FI
AND
GOD BLESS

A Soldiers Whisper
From The Ground

A soldiers whisper
From the ground

A soldiers whisper
From the ground
Will move the hearts
And souls
From all around
When you hear his words
From the ground...
For it is not time
For me to rest
Because my duty here
Is still not done...
All because
My fellow brothers and sister
Are still not home
And the price
Of a soldiers life
Is still to come
Even when I heard those words
From the ground above
In which I lay
That simply said
For this is a debt
That we cannot repay...
And so this is the price
Of our freedom today
All because
Of soldiers like them
That have gave
The ultimate cost
Time and time again
Just
To keep us free...
But now
I have got to go
To prepare another place
For soldiers like me

As they bring
Another one home...
So please
Take a good look around
And you will see
This is the price
That lies at our feet...
For your freedom today
With only the whispers
From the ground...
And you might
Hear them say:
My duty
Is still not done
Even
As they cover the ground
In which I lay
So beneath your feet...
Lays honor
And pride
With the hearts
And souls
Of a soldier cry....

It Is Time

There Is A Time
For Everything
A Time To Honor
And A Time To Respect
Our Hometown Vets
But There Is
No Other Time
Than The Time
At Hand
To Say Thank You
To All Our Vets.

THANK YOU
AND
GOD BLESS

A Fighting Battle

You never really
Get over the things
From your past
You just try
To block them out
So that you
can survive
And carry on
With your life

But they will always remain
In the back of your mind
For years to come
As you truly struggle to survive
and overcome
The things from your past

And for the battles
That you will fight
Each and every day
Of your life

They too
will make you strong
Stronger than before
So that you
Can overcome
the obstacles
That are at hand

But still yet
You will have to fight to survive
the things
That are still
to come

For these
are whole lot more
Than just a battle
That I have fought

And won!
As I still struggle
To carry on
With my life...

THE ROAD I TRAVEL

The road I travel
Is made of turns
Like left turns
Right turns
And U-turns

It has many lanes
Like four lanes
Two lanes
And even
Down to
a one lane road
With only
Oneway to go

It has all kinds
Of bends
And curves
With ups
And downs
And all around

So its from
the dirt roads
To the back roads
From the city streets
To the highways
And even
Onto the interstate

But it's a strange thing
When you find yourself
At the dead end
Of a road

For then
You just gotta
Turn around
And back track
And then

You gotta start
All over again

For these
Are the roads
That I travel
As I travel
Down the road

But is this really
A road that I travel
Or is this a path
A path of life
That helps us grow
As we travel down
Our own road

SSGT Ralph Lee Butler, Jr.

Thank a vet

Never give up an opportunity
To thank a veteran
For you may never
have that opportunity again.

For they
Might not ever
have heard those words
until this today

So for the price
of our freedom
Let us take this opportunity
to remember
and to thank
our Veterans

Because this
is the ultimate cost
of our freedom

Do not judge

Don't Judge The Path
Of My Journey...
If You Haven't Walked
The Journey Of My Path...

IN THE ACTS OF VALOR

IN THE ACTS OF VALOR
THERE IS STILL HOPE
ALL BECAUSE
OF THE ACTIONS
FROM THERE BOLDNESS
AND FROM THERE
DETERMINATION
WHEN FACING GREAT DANGER
ESPECIALLY IN BATTLE FIELDS
WITH HEROIC COURAGE
AND BRAVERY
ABOVE ALL THINGS
SO WITH THE ACTS OF VALOR
THAT HAVE BEEN SERVED
AS ONE OF MY BROTHERS
HAVE FALLEN
TO THE CASUALTIES OF WAR
FOR IT MIGHT NEVER
OF BEEN SEEN
EXCEPT FROM HIS UNIT
WHICH HOLDS
A HIDDEN VALOR
DEEP WITHIN
HIS OWN TEAM
SO FROM THE ACTIONS
OF THE BATTLES
THAT THEY HAVE FOUGHT
THIS IS THERE DUTY
WITH HONOR
AND WITH PRIDE
AS THEY DO IT WITH VALOR
SO FROM THE BATTLES
IN WHICH WE FIGHT
WE NEED NO MEDALS
OR RIBBONS
TO TELL YOU
WERE WE'VE BEEN
BECAUSE
THEY ARE MARKED
AND EMBEDDED

IN OUR HEARTS
AND IN OUR MINDS
FOREVER
EVEN AS THE NIGHTMARES
REMIND US
IN WHERE WE'VE BEEN
BUT WE WILL ALWAYS STAND
TRUE
TO OUR BROTHERS
ALL THE WAY
TO THE END
BUT TIME
AND TIME AGAIN
IT WILL BE DONE
WITH ONLY
THE ACTS OF VALOR
FOR IT IS DONE
AS WE SAY TO EACH OTHER
WE ARE A UNIT
A UNIT OF ONE
AND THIS VALOR
WILL ALWAYS LIVE
WITHIN THE HEARTS
AND THE SOULS
OF OUR KIND
SO THE VALOR
YOU TALK ABOUT TODAY
WILL NEVER BE SEEN
EXCEPT IN A UNIT
OR A TEAM
WHEN IT IS DONE
SO THE MEDAL OF VALOR
OR THE MEDAL OF HONOR
SHOULD ALWAYS BE GIVEN
TO THE KIA
FOR THIS
IS HIS VALOR
WHICH HE HAD SACRIFICED
IN THE LINE OF DUTY
AND THIS IS ABOVE
AND BEYOND
ANYTHING

THAT ANYONE
COULD HAVE EVER DONE

SEMPER-FI
IN THE UNIT
OF A TEAM
FIGHTING
AS ONE

SSGT RALPH LEE BUTLER, JR.

I Still Have To Fight
Just To Survive The Pain

As my heart bleeds
All in pain
I shall not feel
Such a thing
As I bite the bullet
And endure the pain
For I will not
Be defeated
Because my heart
Is still beating
As I try endure
What life has to bring
And with ever beat
That it takes
I know now
That I will live
And survive
Another day
As I try to endure
And overcome
Such a pain
And with ever breath
That I take
It shall mend the heart
That endures
Such a pain
For this
Is the reason
That I
Am here today
As I write these words and say
No pain
No gain
For this
I am strong
As I try to survive
And overcome
The pain

Deep Inside Yourself

Your Pride
Reflects Your Honor
And Your Honor
Reflects Your Pride
All From That
In Which You Hold
And Carry
From Deep Inside

TO HONOR WITH PRIDE

TO HONOR THOSE
WHO HONORED US
IS AN HONOR
ALL
WITH IN IT'S SELF
AND
AS I SERVED
WITH HONOR
THAT HONOR
STILL LIVES
IN MY HEART
AND
IN MY SOUL
FOR THE HONOR
YOU SEE TODAY
IT STANDS BEFORE US
UP
ON A POLE
IN THE SKY
WAVING BACK
IN HONOR
AND
IN PRIDE
SO
IN RETURN
WE'LL SHOW HER
THE RESPECT
THAT SHE HAS EARNED
MAY GOD BLESS HER
AND
KEEP HER SAFE
DAY BY DAY
AND
THREW THE NIGHT
FOR THIS
IS OUR FLAG
OF
THE USA

A Measurement Of Life

Life in its self
should never be measured
by the number
of breaths
that one will take

But it should be
measured
by the things
that takes our breath away

For then
we might be able
to measure the things
that life has to bring

But some
are still to be seen
in the years to come

So remember
the measurement of life
is in the eyes
of the beholder
from that
in which he see's
as it takes
his breath away

The Wall of Fame

For the wall of fame
Has no shame
For it is written
All in my name
With Honor
And with Pride
So come and read
What's on the wall
The Wall of Fame

That's my Daddy

For the man
that is before us
He has been a messenger of peace
For many of years

For many
Have looked upon him
As a born leader
As he stands

He has always been
The mediator
In my life
Being so steady and calm

For he makes no enemies
In where he goes

He keeps his life so neat
And very well organized
Throughout the years

He is so aggressive
and strong
As he prepares himself
For any challenges
That are at hand

For he has had
A positive attitude
That many have seen
Even
Still today
As his memories
Will never fade away

For this
is my daddy
That you have known
Throughout the years
At Macomb

A TASTE OF HER NATURE
IS A SIGHT TO SEE

For I have walked
in her beauty
as I have tasted
her nature
from the rivers
of her valleys
to the streams
of her mountains

From dusk to dawn
I have smelt her beauty
as I have felt
her nature
time and time again
threw the wind
and the air
I have felt the mist
of her waterfalls

Even
as the weather
has changed
From blankets of snow
that has covered the land
to the frozen streams
and the rivers below
I have seen her beauty
at her best
Even
As she changed
like so

So now
I can truly say
that I have lived
within her beauty
But only
for a short while

So it is said
that her beauty
will always live
in the hearts
and in the minds
of those
that have walked
in the valleys below

So because of this
there is a place
that I love go
As I close my eyes
To rest
my body and soul

Because her beauty
brings me peace
no matter
were I may go

But yet her beauty
will never be tamed or ever be told

For it is in the minds and the hearts of
those
that have seen her beauty
that are really told

So
I shall never forget
what my eyes have seen
because her beauty
shall always live
in my memories
from deep within

For this
is the beauty
and the nature
that I have seen
Only In Yosemite

STANDING ON MY OWN
SO TAKE A STAND
AND STAND WITH ME

For there was a time
Back in the day
When I learned to crawl
Then
As I learned to stand
I also
learned to walk around
On my own two feet

So go ahead
And think about this
As you will remember
Back then
When you
Knocked me down
Time and time again
But you must remember
That I was never out

Because
I still remember
This right here
Back in the day
When I was young
In how
I learned to crawl
and stand
As I did
A long time ago

So never
Ever
Count me out
For I
am not done

Because my past
Has made me strong
Stronger
Than you will ever know....

So go ahead
And take
A good look around
Just one more time
And you will see
Me
Standing there...

And then
You will hear me say
You knocked me down
Time
and time again
But I
Was never out
For my will
Will always be
Stronger than you
Stronger
Than you
Will ever be....

For I
Am still standing
Standing right here
Before you
TODAY....

And I will stand
For those
Who can not stand
But one day
They too
Will also stand
As they
Stand with me.......

I WILL SURVIVE

I WILL NOT BE DEFEATED
FOR MY HEART IS STILL
BEATING
AND I AM STILL BREATHING

Search Yourself

If you search your heart
Then your soul
Will be fulfilled

But
If you search your soul
Then your heart
Will be fulfilled

So
No matter
What you search
You will always
Have to search
Your heart and soul

Just
To find some peace
That lays
With in yourself

But only
If you search
Your heart and soul

For then
You will find
All the answers
That you
Will ever need
That has been hidden
For so long
In your heart
And in your soul

But only
If you choose
To search
Your own heart
and soul

Written by
Ralph L Butler Jr
Rowdy

STANDING STRONG

If you do not
stand up for yourself...
or for the things
that you believe in...

Then you will never
be able to stand
for anything at all...
Even when it comes
to yourself...

So remember this
As one would say...

When and if...
You ever stand up
for yourself...
Or for the things
that you believe in...

Thats when others from around you
will stand up
beside you...

Just because
you are strong
Strong enough
To stand up
for the things
That you believe in...

And together
We will be strong...
When all we stand
And come together...

TATTERED AND TORN

I CAN SURVIVE
WHAT EVER YOU BRING
SO GO AHEAD
AND BRING IT ON
THEN WATCH ME
AS I TAKE A STAND
AS I SHOW MY COLORS
ALL ACROSS THIS LAND
SO NOW
TAKE A GOOD LOOK AGAIN
BEFORE YOU EVEN TRY
TO BRING IT ON
BECAUSE
YOU WILL SEE ME
AS LOOK AROUND
AND IT'S LIKE I SAID
I TOLD YOU ONCE
AND I WILL TELL YOU AGAIN
I WILL SURVIVE
AS I TAKE A STAND
ALL ACROSS THIS LAND
SO
I MIGHT BE OLD
BUT I AM SO BOLD
I MIGHT BE TORN
BURNT AND SCARED
BUT IT SHOWS A CHARACTER
IN WHERE I'VE BEEN
FOR THIS
IS JUST PART
OF MY HISTORY
AND A STORY
IN WHERE I'VE BEEN
SO PLEASE GO AHEAD
AND BRING IT ON
AND AGAIN
I WILL SHOW YOU
THAT I WILL SURVIVE
AS I FLY WITH PRIDE
AND HONOR
IN THE SKY

What Do You See

THERE IS PEACE
EVERYWHERE YOU LOOK
IF YOU ONLY
OPEN UP YOUR EYES
SO THAT YOU CAN SEE
THAT WHICH SURROUNDS
YOU AND ME

BUT IF YOU WOULD JUST OPEN
YOUR EYES
AND YOUR HEARTS
AT THE SAME TIME
THEN YOU WILL FIND MORE
THAN YOU HAVE EVER
BARGAINED FOR

BUT ONLY
IF YOU TRULY
WANT TO SEE
THAT WHICH SURROUNDS
YOU AND ME

BECAUSE
THIS WILL BE
A HEART FELT MOMENT
THAT ONLY WE
WILL EVER SEE
OR FEEL
FOR THE REST OF OUR LIVES
AS WE OPEN OUR HEARTS
AND OUR MINDS
TO THAT
OF WHAT WE SEE

FOR THEN
IT CAN ONLY BE
THAT WHICH IS PEACE
THAT WE
WILL EVER SEE
THAT SURROUNDS
YOU AND ME

THATS HER THEME:

I AM A ROLE MODEL
ALL ACROSS THIS LAND
AND NOT SOME KIND
OF A BIKINI THING
THAT LAYS HALF NAKED
IN THE SAND
BUT I WILL STILL PLAY
IN THE DIRTY AND THE SAND
JUST TO PROTECT THIS LAND
FOR THERE IS NO TIME
FOR ME TO LAY
ON THE BEACHS
OF THE SAND
SO THAT I CAN TAN
FOR I AM A ROLE MODEL
A FEMALE
THAT PROTECTS THIS LAND
SO NO CLEAVAGE HERE BOYS
JUST A WEAPON
IN MY HAND
NO FANCEY JEWLRY
MADE OF GOLD
BUT A SET OF DOGS
THAT ARE SO BOLD
FOR I AM THE DAUGHTER
OR THE MOTHER
THAT SERVES
TO PROTECT THIS LAND
SO WHAT YOU SEE
IS WHAT YOU GET
AND TRUST ME BOYS
WHEN I SAY
YOU HAVE NOT
SEEN
NOTHING YET
BECAUSE I SERVE MY COUNTRY
AND I SERVE IT WELL
FOR I AM THE PRIDE
THAT YOU WILL SEE
ALL INSIDE

BECAUSE WE
ARE THE ROLE MODELS
OF PRIDE AND HONOR
FOR YEARS TO COME
AS WE SERVE
TO PROTECT THIS LAND
WITH OUR UNCLE SAM

**From the children
Of Sandy Hook
Elementary School**

As you read my name.
Remember to pray,
for my family
and my friends.
Because we
are now safe
and out
of harms way
as we play
with angels
Right here
in heaven...
Today

Charlotte Bacon,
02-22-06

Daniel Barden,
09-25-05

Olivia Engel,
07-18-06

Josephine Gay,
12-11-05

Ana M. Marquez-Greene,
04-04-06

Dylan Hockley,
03-08-06

Madeleine F. Hsu,
07-10-06

Catherine V. Hubbard,
06-08-06

Chase Kowalski,
10-31-05

Jesse Lewis,
06-30-06

James Mattioli,
03-22-06

Grace McDonnell,
11-04-05

Emilie Parker,
05-12-06

Jack Pinto,
05-06-06

Noah Pozner,
11-20-06

Caroline Previdi,
09-07-06

Jessica Rekos,
05-10-06

Avielle Richman,
10-17-06

Benjamin Wheeler,
09-12-06

Allison Wyatt,
07-03-06

And we the staff
will remain
right here
With your loving children
As we still
Take watch

And look over them...
Each and every day

Rachel Davino,
07-17-83

Dawn Hochsprung,
06-28-65

Anne Marie Murphy,
07-25-60

Lauren Russeau,
06-?-82

Mary Sherlach,
02-11-56

Victoria Soto,
11-04-85

Mommy-Daddy
You where right
When you said
I was your little angel
Because
you should see
my little wings...
Got to go now
Love you always
Your little angel...
So please
don't cry anymore
Cause Jesus said
I'm in good hands now
So please
don't cry for me
For we
are all ok
Right here
In heaven
Today

AMEN.....

Written by
The heart
and the hands
Of a hidden angel

Ralph L Butler Jr
Rowdy

I cried many of years
Waiting and waiting for you
To come back into my life
Fighting off others
Trying to prove to them
Over
and over again
Saying
That you are coming back
But you never did
So now
The tears are gone
And will fall no more
All because I am grown
As I stand here
All on my own
For you know nothing
Nothing at all
About the son
That you left behind
So let it be just that
The son that you left behind
For you are not worth the tears
That had fallen
From the past
For I was just to young to see
Or even know
What kind of a person
That you really where
But now I see
And I'm better off
The way the things had come to be
For you know nothing at all
About me...
From a child
To a man
That came to be

TEACHERS....

TEACHERS ARE MORE
THAN JUST TEACHERS
THEY ARE LIKE GUARDIAN
ANGELS
TRYING TO PROTECT
AND SHIELD
OUR CHILDREN
THAT MAY COME
IN HARMS WAY
AS THEY GROW OLDER
TO BECOME
TEACHERS
THEMSELVES
IN A WORLD
THAT CAN BE
SO RUDE
AND HATEFUL
IN SO MANY WAYS
SO STOP
AND TAKE THE TIME
TO THANK A TEACHER
FOR TEACHING YOU
SO MANY THINGS
THAT YOU TOO
WILL TEACH OTHERS
ALONG THE WAY
FOR WE
ARE JUST TEACHERS
FROM AMONG TEACHERS
TRYING TO PROTECT
OUR CHILDREN
ALONG THE WAY
TEACHERS....

Written by
Ralph L Butler Jr
Rowdy

PLACES TO GO

There is a time
When one will say
I got places to go
And people to see
Even if you don't
Want to see me
For I still
Got places to go..

STUCK ON YOU

YOUR IN MY MIND
YOUR IN MY HEART
AND YOUR IN MY SOUL
SO KNOW MATTER
HOW FAR I GO
OR HOW CLOSE
I MIGHT BE
REMEMBER
THAT YOU
WILL ALWAYS BE
RIGHT HERE
WITH ME
IN MY MIND
AND IN MY HEART
FOR YOU ARE THE AIR
THAT I BREATH
THAT GIVE ME LIFE
AS I BREATH

TODAY

Today I saw a man
A soldier
from our past
For he wore a hat
That made me proud
And the words did say
VETERAN
WORLD WAR II
For we do not see
many veterans
from that era anymore
But I was proud
To see him
standing there
So as a veteran too
I stood there
with honor
And pride
as he stood beside me
A peace of history
Before my eyes
So I showed him
the respect
That he has earned
And Then
I paid for his meal
As little
as it might be
He told me
that I did not have to do that
but I said
It is my honor
And my privilege
To do this
for you today
Because
it is from
one soldier
to another
Then a tear

fell from his face
As we shook hands
And parted our ways

Remember
to thank a veteran
Not only today
But every day

Semper-Fi

A LONE WOLF

There is a time
When you think
You find something
That is so great
in your life
That you want to be apart of
Because it fulfills
apart of your needs
and it helps you find
an enter peace
From your past
But then
you find out
the hard way
Just like
many times before
That they too
will let you down
For its all about
politics groups and clicks
So if you don't fit in
you got to realize
If you want to play
the game
of the clicks and things
Then you got to play there game
That means
you got to give up
On the things that you believe in
Just to be
apart of such a thing
So is it worth the effort
Just to play there game
But put all things aside
And you got to remember
Who you really are
So be proud
And take your stand
And keep going on
with what you believe in

Because you do not
have to play
any of those games
With the clicks and things
But if you would be yourself
Then you will not
get caught up
in the clicks of things
But then
you might be labeled
as the outcast
a lone wolf
As it may be
But that
is just fine for me
Because
I will always have
my freedom
That is at hand
To speak my mind
As I stand alone
As that lone wolf
or even
as an outcast
as it may be
Because I will not play
In the clicks of the games
Because I am me
And I will survive
Just like I have before
In so many ways
But with only
A few more scares
So Thank You —
From a Lone Wolf
as it may be
or even
as it is seen...

Written by
Ralph L Butler Jr
Rowdy

PARENTS

Your parents
Do not
have to have
The same DNA
From which
you are raised
For you to be
A apart
of the family
You just
have to have
LOVE
For each other
As you are raised
From that family
For you
are the same person
DNA
or no DNA
You are still
Of the same
In the family

TEACHING

IS THE KNOWLEDGE
AND THE WISDOM
FROM MANY MEN
HOPING
THAT ONE DAY
SOMEONE
WILL UNDERSTAND
IT'S KNOWLEDGE
AND IT'S WISDOM
THAT HE HIMSELF
HAS LEARNED
FROM THE WISDOM
OF OTHERS
SO SHARE YOUR KNOWLEDGE
AND YOUR WISDOM
AS WELL..
SO THAT MANKIND
MIGHT LEARN SOMETHING
FROM ITS OWN...

Written by
Ralph L Butler Jr
Rowdy

TRUE LEADERSHIP

There Is A Time
When Leadership Falls
But Then Someone
Steps Forward
To Take Charge
And Lead Us All
For That Is When
True Leadership
Will Lead Us All

Written by
Ralph L Butler Jr
Rowdy

Speak up
And be a leader
Don't hide
behind the walls
Of a computer
Stand up
And let your voice
be heard
And let yourself be seen
As true leader...

Never be ashamed
Of the scars
That you have
For it shows a caracter
In where you've been
And it really shows
The strength
That you have
In your life
As you carry on
So hold your head up
And say out loud
I can
And I will
Survive
Even as the scars
Still live
Deep inside
As I carry on
With my life

NEVER ALONE

If you think
you ever
stand alone
Stop
and take
a good look around
And you will see
There are many
That you never
Really knew
That will stand
beside you
When it is time
And say
You are not alone
Because
we can see
what is going on
And you will be
just fine
For you are not alone
So remember
The strength
of one
Bares the strength
of many
For it is not seen
Until it is time
So remember
you are never
really alone
Even as we stand
In the shadows
Of the dark
For we
are always there
So that you
Are not alone
And for what is written
On the wall

you know now
That you
are not alone

Written by
Ralph L Butler Jr
Rowdy

Just To Brag

Some people
will brag about
there lives

Or some people
will brag about
there wives

And some people
will never brag
at all

Just because
they have nothing
to brag about

So
let me brag
about my life
and most of all
my wife

For she is my life
that I can brag about

Because she is my pride and joy
And most all
My best friend

For she
is the reason
Why
I get to brag
about my life

Because
she is my life
That I love to brag about

But
if you asked her
about me
She would say
All he does
Is nag nag nag
and nag
More than
he will ever brag

SSGT RALPH LEE BUTLER, JR.

STRENGTH FROM GOD

He gives me pride
So I don't hide

He gives me strength
So I can stand

He gives me everything
That I
Will ever need

That's what he gives me
When I pray
And talk to him

But can you tell me
The last time you said
Thank you
Thank you Dear Lord
Or
Thank you GOD
For making me
Who I am

For they
Are the ones
That gives me strength
To carry on

In all the things
That I may do

For this
Is more than a reminder
That I can share
With you

For this
Is the strength
That only comes
From GOD

A DEAD END...

Remember my friend
Whenever
You hit
A dead end
There is always
Another solution
To that dead end
So go ahead
And look again
Because there is
No dead end
But just
An excuse
To stop you
From succeeding
In the end...
So now
You can say
There is no end
In
A dead end...

The cost
of our freedom
Is written
on the wall
As it is imbedded
In the hearts
And the souls
Of all of those
That where their
So let it not
Go in-vain
As you defend
What is left
Of her today...
Because this my friend
Is more
than a reminder
As it still lives
In the shadows
Of the dark
and
in the hearts
And the souls
Of our kind
So remember this
As you fought
To survive
And stay alive
From that
which is
Of nothing
but a kill zone
Because now
the wounds
Have just begun
As they turn
Only to scars
That will never mend
For they
Are with you
Forever...
And I do mean
Forever...

To that
in which I have
Let no man
take it
But let me
be kind enough
To share it....

SSGT Ralph Lee Butler, Jr.

Strangers we are
For we
Have never meet
But friends
We'll be
Until the time
That we have meet...
For then
It will be
Like a family reunion
When we all
Get to meet
And say
We are more
Than just friends
And we are more
Than just family
For it is something
That I can not explain
Even
To the end....

TILL DEATH DO US PART

The day
I took your hand
Is the day
I promised you
a life of adventure
And throughout the years
I gave to you
Just that
But we had
our ups
and downs
Along the way
Just like
So many do
But we stuck together
To the end
And now
That its almost over
our love
Will always live
in our children
And from the things
That we have
Even thou
I am gone
You still hold
The love I have
In your heart
and in
your loving hands
But one day
And one day soon
We will be
Together again
Just you and me
And they will see
The love
That we truly have
From back in the day
When I took
your loving hand

If you teach someone
Something that you know
Always remember
That they too
Can teach you something
Just as well
About something
That you did not know...

YOUR BIBLE...

Someone once said...
You need to get a bible
So I did...

Them someone told me...
That I need
to get a family bible
So I did...

Then someone told me...
I need to put
the family bible
in the living room
So I did...

Then someone told me...
That I need
to put a bible
by my bed
And so I did...

But then one day
A stranger
came to me
Just out of the blue
And said
Where is you bible
my son...

And I looked at him
in a very strange way
As I said
In my living room
And by my bed

But then
he asked me
Have you ever
read the bible

And I just said No
I have never
read the bible
For I was just told
to get a bible
And so I did
Then I was told
to get a family bible
And so I did
Then I was told
to set the family bible
in my living room
And so I did
Then I was told
to put the other
by my bed
And that's
what I did...

Then the stranger
looked at me
and said
Clear the dust
from your bible
and read my words
For my name is JESUS
And you my son
Will truly
get to know me
From your bible...
That you
will now read
And go ahead
tell others
About me...
And that
of the story
Of Your Bible...

MY FIRST LOVE...

I will always wonder
If you remember
The reflection
Of that today
Because you held more
Than my heart
As we spent time together
On that beautiful day...
But then at sunset
We had to go
So we kissed
And said goodbye
But I still came back
Each and every day
As I sat here
on that dock
Where we meet
But all alone
Waiting for you
To just come back
But you never did
Because cancer
Took you away...
For life its self
is not fare
And they said
I was just to young
To really care
Or even know
What love
is really about
But they where wrong
because you my dear
Showed it to me
In many ways...
For you
Are my first love
That I will remember
For years to come
Even to

my last days...
As cancer now
Takes me away...
So close your eyes
And you will find
A reflection
Of her and I
Sitting right here
On the dock
With our arms around
one anther
Each and every day
And now I know
With out a doubt
That you remember
That beautiful day...
As you bring me
the same flowers
That I gave to you
On that day...

He will answer

Just because
he does not answer you
right away...
Doesn't mean
that he didn't hear you...
It's because
He is giving you time,
to think about it....
But if
you don't figure it out,
then he will answer you
in due time...
For this
Is just another lesson
that comes from god...

LET THE WINDS
OF MY VESSEL
GUIDE ME
TO THE TREASURES
THAT I SEEK...

Written by
Ralph L Butler Jr
Rowdy

THE HIDDEN TREASURES
MARKED ONLY
BY AN X

The pirates
of me ship
my lad
Will obey
what I say
Or walk the planks
And the sharks
will be feed
For that's the life
Of the pirates
My lad
Now onto sea
And be like me
With a dream
And a fortune
of a pirates gold
That lays
In me chest
That is marked
By an X
that we my lad
will seek
With jewels
Of ruby's
And gold
Set forth
With a kings crown
Which is
of gold
For it is all
that we seek
From the treasures
Of the map
Marked only
by an X
Arrrrr
So buried treasures
That are of gold

For that's
another day
So from the riches
of the king
Shall be
the riches
of the poor
That I truly seek
Now drink
from me jug
And say
That's all mine
and it all belongs
to me
The chest of gold
That we seek...
Marked only
By an X
Is all
That we seek....
Arrrrr my lad
Arrrrr

THE THRESHOLD

THE THRESHOLD
OF OUR PEOPLE
WILL COME TOGETHER
FROM A SPIRIT
IN THE STRONGHOLD
WHEN THE TIME
IS RIGHT
AS WE FIND
A NEW LEADER
TO LEAD OUR PEOPLE

It's a sacred place
where you will go
To find the spirit
Of your grandfathers
With great wisdom
And knowledge
That you will gain
As you learn
From the spirits
As they are joined
and become of one
As they touch
your heart and soul
And they
will give you
An enter peace
With strength
And understanding
from the blood
Of our people
But only
if you seek the truth
Will you see that
Of the great spirit
That you truly seek
From that
Of a thousand years
When you enter
the threshold

Of our people
As they guide you
to the stronghold
That you seek...
But only
If your heart is pure
Will you see
and find the answers
To that
of what you truly seek
As you stand
in the stronghold
Of our people
With the spirits from the past
As you get your answers
From that
of what you truly seek...

WORDS FOR THOUGHT

Respect other people's rights
As you would wish them
To respect yours...

Someone once said
Did you ever serve
a single day
in the military
And I had to reply
and say no
For I have never served
a single day
in my life
Because
I have served
a life time
As I still serve
Even today
And for the scares
that I carry
are just
from yesterday
So ask me again
And I will say
Now
you tell me
What do you think

A moment of memory

If you see something
That takes your breath away
Cherish that moment forever
Because in a blink of an eye
It has already changed
And it will never
Be of the same...
For it is already gone...

A BROTHER IN ARMS...

You are now
On another mission....
A mission that will be
Like that of no other...
And without a doubt
Honor Pride Dignity
and Respect
Will be given
When they bring
Another one home...
And the sound will require
That of taps
When he
comes back...
But for now
my brother
Take a brake
And try to rest
For the time is near
When they will bring
Another one home...
But we are still
That of a unit
A unit of one
As we served together
Like so many have done
With only
One objective
One thought
One mission
In one mind
With that
Of one shot
That still haunts us
As it takes us back
To that of the time
With nothing
But a flash back
As we close our eyes...
To try to forget
And then we take
A deep breath

As we try
to clear the tears
From that of our eyes
As we tell ourselves
Time and time again
That was then
And now is now
For we did it
To stay alive
And we must
Carry on
For we can not go back
In that of time
But we can
And we will...
Carry on
As we Survive
As we still try
To carry on
From that of the past
But we still
struggle
Each and every day
With that
Of every loss
That comes our way
And with a sacrifice
Like this
Of just one...
Is still
One to many...
When they come home...
In a body bag
Like this...
As our memories
Will never rest...
As we lay
Another hero
To rest...

Written by
SSGT Ralph L Butler
Rowdy

A HEART OF PAIN...

There is something
about me
and my life
That I can explain
Or understand
How I feel the pain of others
Before I ever
feel the pain of mine....
And how
this ever came to be...
Except maybe
Because I told my self
Time and time again
that others
had it harder
than me...
As I became
An expendable item
And just maybe
That's how
I came to be...
From one foster home
To another
And then again
To another
And then another...
And so on
down the line
Until the day
That I made my way...
To something
That I still today
can not understand
Or explain
All because
I can not
And will not
Walk away....
From that
Of your pain...

Written by
Ralph L Butler Jr
Rowdy

THE PEN

A pen
And paper
Will always
Go together
But without the ink
They are nothing
As the words go blank...
For there is nothing to read
Or even write...
Because the pen itself
Has gone dry...
With no words to read
or even write...
So much
Like the heart
And the soul
From within yourself
As you share the words
From your heart
That you write...

Written by
Ralph L Butler Jr
Rowdy

A road not traveled
Is a path not seen...
But only
In that of your dreams

A Sgt. once said
Can you
Handle the pressure
And being
The smart ass
That I was
I sort of giggled
In my own way
As I said yes
I could handle the pressure
But then
The day had come
When I lost a soldier
A brother
And a friend
All in one
As I lost control
Of myself
And took the life
Of another....
All in the same day
And then
I started to realized
That the hate
and the anger
Has a different kind of pressure
Which holds
A whole different meaning....
So next time
When a Sgt says
Can you handle the pressure
You better think twice
Before you answer that question...
Because the blood
Never goes away
And the tears themselves
Are still hidden
And tucked away
Deep in the soul
And covered in pain
As it will never
Go away...

From the memories
That you'll carry
For the rest of your life
All from that
of yesterday....
As you try
To hold yourself together
Each and every day....
For this is truly a battle
That no one
Will ever win....
As the memories still flash
Before your own eyes...
And this
Is the hidden pressure
That no one
Seems to tell you about...
From the lives
That you took
To the lives
That you lost
That are now hidden
In the memories
Within yourself...

SSGT RALPH LEE BUTLER, JR.

A SIMPLE PHRASE...
IS NOT AS SIMPLE
AS YOU THINK...

There seems to be
One line above another
That we will change
With that of another...
But then again
There might be
One line below another
That we
will want to change
With that
of another...
That is still
just as good
As the other
But if we changed
them around
With something
of another
Will we ever
Be satisfied
With just that
of the other
Because it may never
read the same
If we change it
with another...

Written by
Ralph L Butler Jr
Rowdy

A TRUE MEANING
OF MEMORIAL DAY

I know with out a doubt
That you've heard a song
About a soldier
That comes to mind
For his name
Will not go in shame
For it is written
In that of stone
Somewhere
Right here
In Arlington
At the national cemetery
That all can see
From a line of headstones
Dressed
In a formation
And with flags themselves
In a colorful line
Like that of no other
That many
Have come to see
And really
Knows nothing
About me
And somewhere
From among those ranks
You will see his name
In that in which you seek
Or maybe
On that wall
That you dare to see
As the memories
Begin to flash
Just like that
With that of a picture
Of my brothers
Standing
side by side
In a reflection

Of a mirror
Like no other
That still remains
On that very wall
With over
58,272 names
That are engraved
And imbedded
On this very wall
And still
There are more to come
As the names
Of the soldiers
Are added
On Memorial Day
One by one
To this wall
So all I can do
Is hope and pray
That one day
It will come
To a rest
As the tears themselves
Begin to fall
From our eyes
Just like that
Because of the memories
That we still have
From that of our past
So time
and time again
Many will come
And many will pass
As they read the names
Of these brothers
From the past
As we remember
One another
On this very day
As we drive along
With the memories
That we hold on to
From that of our past...
So I salute you

My brother
My dear friend
As we lower that flag
To half mast
In memory of you
And all the others
Just alike
Right here
On Memorial Day
As I stand here
Weak in the knees
Wondering why
And just how
This really
came to be
As I still fight
the memories at night
And I try
To hold back those tears
When it comes
To this very day
As I see you
And some others
Standing
On the other side...
Saluting
And waving back
Telling us
It's ok
As we shed this honor
Back and forth
To one another....
With pride
And respect
To that
Of no other....
When it comes
To Memorial Day

Rowdy-Man
The Oklahoma Poet
May 26, 2013

Always cherish
what you got today
for you never now
what tomorrow holds
Before it all
Just slips away...

As life comes along
You really never know
Just where to stand
But you still find a place
As you overcome
And adapt...

As the words
from my heart
are spoken
Let them tell
of the hidden words
that are unspoken

At the break of dawn
In the morning light
The sun will rise
And heat
the morning skies
As it warms the hearts
and the soul
From deep inside
As we all wait upon
The morning star...
Just to rise
And once again
She will set
In the evening skies...
With the memories
That will last
A life time
All from that
of what we see
As the day itself
Seems to slip away
And goes right on by
But a view
will still remain
in our hearts
And in our minds
As they come to rest
in our souls
as we close
and rest our weary eyes...
Until that
Of another day...

Close your eyes
And hear the whispers
Of my voice
And tell me
What is it
That you truly see
As you draw a picture
To your own conclusion
To something
That may never be
Except maybe
In that of your dreams
Or can it be
Something
That is not of a dream...
So tell me again
What is it
That you truly see
When you close your eyes
And hear the whispers
Of my voice...
Coming through the leaves
And the branches
Of those trees
As it seems to echo
In that of the winds
As it carries me
From the mountains above
To the valleys below
As the whispers themselves
Seems to come
To that of an end
Somewhere
Out at sea...
Until that
Of another day
When it rides the waves
Back to the shore
And begins to whisper
All once more
With that of a journey
To no end

As we all begin
To listen in
To the whispers
That have come to shore
That holds a secret
Of a single whisper
That now rest
In our hands
As we try again
To listen in...
As the secrets themselves
Still echo around
In those very winds...
That has been captured
In a seashell
That has come to shore...

SSGT RALPH LEE BUTLER, JR.

DON'T JUDGE ME
NOT UNTIL
YOU HAVE STEPPED
INTO MY SHOES
AND HAVE WALKED
JUST PART OF THAT
OF MY JOURNEY...
FOR THEN
YOU WILL KNOW...
JUST WHERE
I COME FROM...
AND JUST ONE QUESTION
WILL REMAIN
CAN YOU SURVIVE
IN THAT OF MY SHOES...
NOW GO AHEAD
AND JUDGE ME...

Written by
Ralph L Butler Jr
Rowdy

Every chair here
is filled with the love
of a lost one
But yet we survive
in the memories
of your hearts...
For we will never
say goodbye...
As you remember
each and everyone of us
On this very day
Of April 19
at 09:01
For this is the day
That I lost you
And went away...
In 1995
But still yet
I am alive
From the memories
That are in you...
From this very day
So don't ever
Let me fade away...
For I am still here
And alive today
With each
and everyone of you
On this very day
In the heartland
Of the USA...

Every journey
into the past
Holds a moment
that seems
to never fade
from that
of our past...

Written by
Ralph L Butler Jr
Rowdy

Follow the road
To that of no end
For that's where the adventure
Will always begin...
When you find yourself
At the trails end...

For the answers
That you seek
Are not always
In black and white
But the answers
Are always there
To that of what you seek...

For the flight I take
Let it be seen
In the darkness
Of the night
As I spread my wings
And fly away....
To that
Of the light...

For The Notes I Keep
Holds The Sacred Words
To That Of What I Seek...
As I Search For Those
That I May Need...
When My Heart
And Soul
Needs To Speak...

The hidden voice
of the whispers

FOR THE WORDS
THAT ARE HIDDEN
DEEP WITHIN YOURSELF...
COMES FROM THE MARKS
THAT ARE HIDDEN
JUST AS WELL...
WHERE THE WORDS
THEMSELVES
ARE ALWAYS LEFT BEHIND
AND NOWHERE
TO BE FOUND...
EXCEPT IN THE SCARS
THAT ARE ALWAYS FOUND...

For Who You Are
Comes A Foundation
That You Have Built
From That
Of Your Past
And So
From That Foundation
Never
Look Back...

Because There Is Nothing
From That Of Your Past
That Is Worth
Looking For
Because This Is Now
Your Foundation
And Not
Of Theirs....
And Your The One
That Built It...
Of Your Own Free Will...
And From That
Of Your Choice...
Now That's
Who You Are...
As You Reach Out
For That
Of The Stars...

Written by
Ralph L Butler Jr
Rowdy

Free As A River...

Free can only be
As free as the water
In that of a river
Or a stream
As it runs free
With that
of another

FROM THAT
OF THE BLOOD
OF MY OWN HANDS...
LET MY PEN
TELL ITS STORY...

From The Cost
Of The Blood
Of Our Own Hands
We Shall Stand
And Fight
For What Is Right
As We Survive
From The Wounds
Of The Past
With That
Of The Hidden Scars...
That Still Seems To Fall
In The Form Of A Tear
With That Of No Fear...
As The Paper Reads
To That
Of My Death...
A Soldier
That Came To Be...
That Is Now
A Silhouette
That You See...

Written by the blood
Of my own hands
SSGT Ralph L Butler Jr
Rowdy

The silhouette

From the darkness
of the shadows
Comes an image
from the light
For there
Will always be
A hidden silhouette
That will show me
The true colors
Of who
You really are...
All from the shadows
Of the darkness
That still lingers
From that of the light...
As the shadows themselves
Come to life...

He hears
Every word
And every prayer
That we
shall ever say
As we speak
And talk to him
But do we
Hear his answers
When he talks
And speaks to us...
As he answers
each and every prayer...
That we
Have ever prayed
As he talks back
To us...

Written by
Ralph L Butler Jr
Rowdy

It never dies

How do you live
With the pain and agony...
In that of your life...
You don't
Because it lives with you...
Every day
Of your life....

How do you touch
the heart of someone
When their heart
is as cold as ice....
Just show them
The blood of yours...
And let the soul of a man
Come to life...
For the answers themselves
Will only come
From that inside...

If there is one bike
There is a hundred
And if there is a hundred
There is a hundred more
But if you look close
You will see
That of a thousand
And a thousand more
For that's who we are...
As we ride in the spirit
Of the PGR...

Written by
Ralph L Butler Jr
Rowdy

I want you
Just to be
My lighthouse
So if I'm lost
I will find you
In the dark of the night
For you
Are my shinning light
As I travel
Threw the day
Or in the night
As the shadows themselves
Are left behind
With nothing
But the shinning
Of pure light
As I follow that
Of my guiding light

If it is our human nature
To live in the light
Then tell me why
We like to dwell
In the darkness
Of the night

If you ever
come face to face
with yourself
then what
will you say
and what
will you do...
Because
It always seems
that no one
likes to face
themselves
even when fronted
by someone else...

If you my friend
Can not understand
The words
That has been written
Then how
Can you understand
The voice
Behind them...
As he reads those words
That he has written...

IT'S A PATH
TO NO END...

When you find yourself
at a trails end
And there is
no other path
to be found
As you look around
Then take the time
And build one
So when others arrive
They will still
have a path to fallow
As they cross that bridge
To a new journey
That has just become
A new trail
To that of a path
Of no end...

Written by
Ralph L Butler Jr
Rowdy

It always seems
That the aftermath
Of a tragedy
Will always bring
Strangers together
In that
Of another way
That many
Have never seen
As they embrace
One another
With the strength
Of each other
From the tragedies
Of today....

IT IS MORE...
THAN JUST A PRAYER...

In the time of prayer
Or even
In the need of prayer
You my friend
Need to remember...
That he is there
As he listens
To that of your prayers...
So feel free
To call upon his name
And I will promise you
That he will be there...
Listening
To each and ever word
In that of your prayers...
For he protected me
In so many ways
That I can not explain
But all
I can truly say
Is this here...
For the man
That you see
That's on the cross
He's not there
Anymore
For he got off
A long time ago
Because he stood with me
So many times
In that of my life
As he heard
Each and every word
To that of my prayers
Or I my friend
Would not be here today
As he answered them
In his own way...
So think again

About the man
That appears to be
On that cross
But remember
He got off
As he now
Stands here with you
On this day
In the time of prayer
When you my friend
Needed him
The most...
For his name
Is JESUS....
THE SON OF GOD
Who will guide you
and protect you
Along the way
When you call
Upon his name...
And JESUS
Will say...
FEAR NOT
FOR I AM WITH YOU...

LIVING FOR TODAY

It really does matter
how you live today
Because yesterday
is just a thing
of the past
And tomorrow
it a thing
of the future
So past present and or future
There is only one
That you can live in
And that my friend
is today...

An escort by an angel

It's Time
To Come Home
And Rest...
So Park Your Rig
And Let Me
Drive You Home
Fear Not
For I
Am With You...
As We Take
This Last Trip...
Amen

JUST A TALK...

If you talk to someone
Talk with them
And then they will listen
But if you talk at someone
They will not listen
Because you do not give them
The undivided attention
That they desire
So if you talk at them
There is no true communication
Until you talk with them....

Protecting those from a fight

Just remember
To hell
And back
We can
And will
Still fight....
Even for those
Who cannot fight...

Enter strength

Just because
You got the heart
And the drive
Does not mean
That you can survive
That of another ride...

The voice of a leader

Let him whisper to me
and let my voice
Be as gentle
as his whisper
But still strong enough
to be heard
As I share that
of his words
That truly
need to be heard
So listen
and you will hear
The words
of his whisper...

Let the light shine on me..

From the darkness of the night
To the light of the day
Let his light shine
And let it shine on me
For I am standing
in his light
Not only by day
But by the night as well
As he shines his light
on me...

Written by
Ralph L Butler Jr
Rowdy

The blood of another

Let us not forget
the blood that has been shed
As we remember our brothers
Here today
But not only
On memorial day
And yes
I must say
We meet as strangers
But we came home as brothers
And all gave some
And some gave all
That we all
come to remember...

True spoken words

Let the truth be told
And hold nothing back
For tears will fall
When the heart hears that...

Life itself
Is just to short
So we all
got to remember
That when
we neglect someone
We also
neglect ourselves
from one
to another...

LOVE IS FOREVER
EVEN WHEN YOU SEE IT
CHISELED IN A STONE...
FOR THEN
YOU WILL KNOW
WITHOUT A DOUBT...
THAT THEIR LOVE
WAS FOREVER...

The hearts
of each other
Are now chiseled
In a foundation
That is made of stone
Right here
Where we now rest...
Side by side
Just like
the first day
That we ever meet...
Together
we will live
Forever
we will be
As we now
lay here
to rest...
In a foundation
That was made
just for us...

Written by
Ralph L Butler Jr
Rowdy

An unspoken prayer

May these words
Comfort you
Through the night
And at the first break
Of light
May you remember
The words
That kept you safe
Through the night
For he is the one
That stood watch
As you slept
Through the night...

Love still grows

Our love
For one another
Is very strong
But I must say
Our love
For each other
Grows stronger
Each and every day...
As my heart
Still falls for you
Like yesterday...
Because I my dear
Am in love with you
And you are the one
That gives me life
And a reason to live
So with every breath
That I take...
Is all because
Of you...
And the love
That we have
For one another
As I say to you
I love you...
More and more
Each and everyday

Power and greed

Power and greed
Comes together
In many ways
Even from those
That we thought
Was our friends
As they look out
Only for themselves...
But as time goes on
That greed
Will reveal its self
As they thrive to feed
On that
That they call
The weak...
So tell me now
Do you feed
On the weak
Or do give strength
To those
That need you most...
Because the strength
Of each other
Can overcome that
Of the power
And the greed
From the others
That try to feed
On that
Of the weak...

Just say thanks

Remember
To take the time
And thank a veteran
While he or she
Is still alive

Because
Without them
We have nothing

For it is the veteran
And not the preacher
Who has given us
The freedom of religion

It is the veteran
And not the reporter
Who has given us
The freedom of the press

It is the veteran
And not the poet
Who has given us
The freedom of speech

It is the veteran
And not the schools
Who has given us
The freedom to assemble

It is the veteran
And not the lawyers
Who has given us
The right to a fair trial

It is the veteran
And not the politicians
Who has given us
The right to vote

For it is the veteran
Who salutes this flag

And it is the veteran
Who serves this flag

And this my friend
Makes me proud
To be an American
And a veteran
Just as well

As we stand
To protect
The constitution
Of the united states
That our four fathers
Have written
And built
From the blood
Of this land

As we protect her
And this flag....
Against all enemies
Foreign
And domestic

For it is written
In the constitution
Of the united states

Those we the people
Have the power
And the right
Not only
To bear arms
But to be free
Just as well....

So it will always be
A veteran

SSGT RALPH LEE BUTLER, JR.

Whose coffin is draped
By this very flag
That he has protected
To this very day

For he
Is a veteran
Of the USA
And this flag
Still proves it
Here today...

My house on the prairie

Ride the prairies
As far as they will take you
But never lose track
Of your camp fire
Because it will give you
A sense of direction
To that of your home
Just as you see
The smoke
From off in the distance
Coming from a cabin
That you will call home
Just as you ride
The open prairies
To that of your dreams
So never loose site
Of the roof top
That comes in site
For it is your home
That sits in the middle
Of the prairie
As you remember those days
Sitting by the camp fire
And all alone
Dreaming about a place
Somewhere
In the middle of the prairie
That you now
Call home...

Just run

Running to someone
Is like a dream
But running to no one
Is nightmare
In that of your dreams...

A friend once said
If you're gonna run
Then run to me
But if you have no friend
Then who
Are you gonna run to...
And where
Will you run....
As you keep running
Nowhere...
With that of nowhere
To hide...

The mark of a scar

Scars
Are just more
Than just scars...

The scars of a man
Is from the struggles
Of that of his life
As he still fights
To survive...
And his scars
Reflect that
Of his life...
As he still fights
To survive
And
To stay alive
Where he himself
Will always
Survive...
And that my friend
Makes me
Who I am...
As I
Take a stand
Once more
With the marks
Of that
Of many scars
That only proves
One thing...
That I can
And I will
Survive
Once more
Just like
So many times
Before...

SSGT RALPH LEE BUTLER, JR.

Some day
I will be able
To walk in your boots
Just like you...
Because I've been watching
and following your footsteps
As I only try
to mimic you
All because
I want to be
Just like you...
But I'm still
Not big enough
At lease not yet
To say those words
That you do
So I guess for now
I'll keep standing here
Next to you...
Until the day
I get as big
and as tall
As you
And then
Maybe
I can be
Just like you
And say those words

I Love You...
To my wife
And kids
Just
Like you...

Some friends
Will stand beside you
All the way
To the end
And some friends
Will do nothing
Until the end..
So really
You are blessed
Threw the thick
and the thin
Because you my friend
Will always have more
Than one friend
At the very end...

What shall I do

Some times
The right thing to do
Is to do nothing at all
And let nature itself
Take its course
But it still seems
That the problem
Still remains
That of the same
As we try
To figure it out
And once again
We'll ask ourselves
Time and time again
What is
The right thing....
As we fight a battle
Within ourselves
Trying
To figure it all out
As we say once more
What is
The right thing...
Because only time
Will ever tell...

The voice of a child will carry in the Oklahoma winds

The cries of our children
Will always remain
In those Oklahoma winds
As they come
And go again
But the memories
Of our children
Will never
Come to an end...
As the storms themselves
Come across
The hearts
Of our land
That we call
The heartland
As we hold those children
In our hearts
And in our hands

SSGT RALPH LEE BUTLER, JR.

The evils of the world
Seems to never end
With hate
And discontent
So that is why
We'll stand here
Protecting those
In a time of need
At their request
As the sound
Of rolling thunder
Rolls to town....
Honoring those
With pride
And respect...

THE FLOW OF THE WATER
IS NEVER THE SAME
WHEN YOU TOUCH THE
WATER
WITH YOUR FINGER TIPS
FOR THEN THE PATH
HAS BEEN CHANGED
AND SO IS THE TIME
FOR IT IS NOT
OF THE SAME...
AS IT PASSES THROUGH
YOUR FINGER TIPS...

So Time
Is Like A River
As It Flows
Through Your Fingers
For You Can Not Touch
The Water Twice
Because The Flow
Of The Water
That Has Passed
Through Your Fingers
Will Never
Pass Again
So Enjoy
Every Moment
Of Your Life
That You Can...
As The Time
Still Flows
Between
Your Finger Tips
Just Like The Water
That Seems To Pass
As It Floats Away
Just Like That
Through Our Own
Finger Tips...
But If There Was
A Thing
From The Past

That We Can Call
A Second Chance
Then What
Would You Hold
From That
Of The Past...
Before
It Flows Through
Your Finger Tips...

Written by
Ralph L Butler Jr
Rowdy

The Heart
And The Soul
Of A Child
That Lays Deep
In Their Mind
As They Mimic
That Of A Soldier
That Stands Behind
For They Do Not Know
Just What They Do
Or Even
What It Truly Means
As They Mimic
Our Salute
Or Do They
Really Know
But Soon
And Soon Enough
They Will Know
As They Remember That
From Yesterday
When They See
Another Child
That Mimics His Salute
Just As He Did
A Long Time Ago
When He Himself
Was A Child Too
And So From This
It Might Be
Just A Mimic
That You See
But What We See
Is Something Different
From That
Of A Salute
From The Heart
And The Soul
That Is Pure
And True
As They Mimic Our Salute
For This

Is The Heart
And The Soul
That Lays Deep
In A Child
That Has Honor
And Pride
As I Too
Will Return His Salute...
To Such A Child...
And It Proves To Me
Just One Thing
That There Is Still Hope
For You And Me...
As We Salute
Each Other
Here Today....

THE HIDDEN VOICE
WITHIN YOURSELF

Whenever
you talk to yourself
And answer back
That is the only time
that you will get
the true answers
from yourself...
As you answer only
to yourself
For its like
A second voice
Heard only
By yourself...

Written by
Ralph L Butler Jr
Rowdy

The memory of time
Will soon pass
Just like the sand
In an hour glass

YOUR DRIVE

THE SECRET TO SUCCESS
WILL ONLY COME
FROM THAT OF YOUR DRIVE...

The silence of the words
Are only spoken from within
As they whisper through your thoughts
Holding nothing
In your hand...
As your mind goes blank
In that of the wind...

The sound of the bikes
As they roar
coming down
some ole road
To a small town
Out in the middle
Of nowhere
Are nothing but angels
That are coming
insight
That God himself
Had sent to you
Through out the night
So on this very day
When you my friend
Needed him most
To comfort you
With that
Of a hundred angels
Dressed in leather
Riding there bikes...
And as they get close
You will see
A patch or two
That will read
Patriot Guard Riders
Riding with Respect
Or one like this
That might read
Standing for those
Who stood for us
And that my friend
Is who we are
And what we do...
So when you see
Or hear the sound
Of that of the roar
Remember
From out in the distance
We will come
All once more
With a hundred bikes...

Or even more
As they rumble and roar
With that
Of the American Flag
Dressed with others
By her side
All to honor
with pride
And respect...
As she speaks out
From that
Of an escort
Whenever
we are needed
To ride...
Or even to hold
A flag line...
For we will be there
In a time of need...
Because we are
The PGR...

Written by
Ralph L Butler Jr
Rowdy

The spirit of a horse
Is not meant to be broken
Neither is the spirit
Of single a child
As they both shall roam
Like the wind
And the rain
That seems
To come and go
All on there own
As they truly please
So let it be
Just like that
From deep within
To that of no end
As they both shall roam
Across this land
With dreams of passion
And the dreams of hope
With the choice to live
To that of there own
That will only come
From deep within
With that of a spirit
That will never be broken
And never be tamed
All because
They are truly free
And all on there own
Like that of an eagle
When she spreads her wings
And takes flight
Like a free spirit
That will only come
From that of there own...

THE TABLE OF KNIGHTS...

Their is one thing
You shall seek
When you come to my table
And that
Is of friendship
with loyalty
Indeed...

Written by
Ralph L Butler Jr
Rowdy

The unheard words
That are still
the unspoken words
From that of yesterday
Are still at bay
For they have not
Yet been written
In anyway
Because they have been hidden
And tucked away
For that of many years
But one day soon
The words will flow
And be heard
As they are written
From that of long ago
So that others
Can read those words
From that of a picture
Or even a phrase
That you will remember
For years to come
All from the words
of yesterday
But can you fathom
That of the words
or that of the phrase
That has been hidden
And tucked away
As they are now
Being written...
For you to see
And read
But only
If you can fathom
What has truly
been written...
For there are still words
That are hidden
In the words
That you
will read....
The unspoken words
Of an abused child

Comes from the heart
and the soul
Of such a child
As they speak
Only with the words
In a form
of a whisper
That cries out
From the heart
And the soul
Of that of a child
As his action
May say it best
When he sits
and plays
by himself
Because he feels left out
and all alone
So can't you see
or even hear
those simple words
That comes out
as a whisper
for they truly
needed to be heard
Because a time like this
is the only time
they may ever
get a chance
to say anything
Before it's to late
to say anything at all
From that of child
That wants to be heard
But just not sure
what to say
As the tears
start to fall
But when and if
they feel safe enough
to say something
They just might
take the chance
If they are away

From that of the threat
and the danger
that they feel
Because they are still
living in fear
Of being hit
for saying something
they should not say
As they speak out
but only with the words
of a whisper
That only they
seem to hear
Because no one
is truly listening
To what they have to say
As they speak out
With silent tears
In that of a whisper
For the tears are hidden
as they fall
from deep inside
So take the time
to just listen
For you might
Just catch a tear
and learn something
From a voice
that just whispers
That will come
From such a child
When they are removed ...
From the threat
And the danger...
Where time itself
Is of the essence...

Written by
Ralph L Butler Jr
Rowdy

The weather will become
Something of its nature
When the storm itself
Decides to come
As it starts
To rumble and roar...
With the sounds
Of no other
When it hits the ground...
And becomes that
Of a storm...

There is something
about me
and my life
That I can explain
Or understand
How I feel the pain of others
Before I ever
feel the pain of mine....
And how
this ever came to be...
Except maybe
Because I told my self
Time and time again
that others
had it harder
than me...
As I became
An expendable item
And just maybe
That's how
I came to be...
From one foster home
To another
And then again
To another
And then another...
And so on
down the line
Until the day
That I made my way...
To something
That I still today
can not understand
Or explain
All because
I can not
And will not
Walk away....

SSGT RALPH LEE BUTLER, JR.

TO THE FOOTSTEPS
OF MY FATHER

For the buried soldier
Beneath this ground
Lays my Daddy
That I come to see...
With a thousand more
That lays beside him
and still I see
A thousand more
That will come...
For I am just a child
Can't you see...
But one day
It will be
That of another child
That will come
And see me...
As we follow the footsteps
Of our fathers...
That come to rest
Right here
With you and me
As history repeats itself
In the footsteps
That we all
Come to see
Right here
In Arlington
At this national cemetery
Where soldiers like him
Will come to be
As we walk those footsteps
To our fathers
And our fathers
Before them....
Don't you see
As they carry me
In the footsteps
Of my family

WHEN A HEART BLEEDS
FOR THAT OF ANOTHER....

If you can feel the pain
from that of others...
Then you have felt
that pain yourself...
From that
of your own...
Or you would not
be able to feel the pain
from that of others...
As the heart still bleeds
For that of others...

Written by
Ralph L Butler Jr
Rowdy

TOGETHER AS ONE

WHEN TWO
BECOME ONE
THEN THATS WHEN LIFE
HAS REALLY BEGUN...

When we raise the flag
There is pride
That comes from inside
And when
She is lowered
To half mast
There is a tear
That comes to our eyes
As memories themselves
Begin to flash
Just like that
Even when
We hear the sound
Of taps
And to that
Of the same
When she is folded
And handed to a mother
Of a fallen soldier
That was
A KIA
And there are more
Still to come
Just like those
From our past
That are MIA's
But they will all
Stand behind
This old flag
Of the USA
All because
Our enlistment
That we took
Has no expiration
So when you see her
Flying high
Remember
There is more
To those colors
That meets the eye...
Because the stars
And the stripes

Holds something
Of our history
That is still alive
As she waves back
At you and I
And let us not
Forget those
That are POW's
When we try
To clear the tears
From our eyes
Hoping
That they too
Are still alive...
As the flag itself
Reminds us
Of just who
We really are...

When you walk
the path of life
Take the time
to live the adventures
Of that
of what you see
For then
you can truly say
I have lived
many of adventures
From the path
of my life...

Written by
Ralph L Butler Jr
Rowdy

WHO ARE YOU...

Now that's
The greatest question
That one
Would ever ask
Of you...

Who are you...

And my answer
To that
Would only be
Just
Like this...

It would take that
Of a life time
For me
To answer a question
Like that...

Because things
Keep changing
In that of my life...

As I too
Will change with them...

Even
As I surprise myself
In that
Of so many ways...

For I have learned
To adapt
To life it self...
And whatever
It brings...

With that
Of the changes
In my life...

But really
I must say
Who are you
To ask me...

For I do not know
What tomorrow brings...

As time it's self
Will change again
And so
Will I...

For that's
Who I truly am...

Or
I can say...

I'm like a river
Flowing
Out to sea

Where my journey
Started
In that
Of a creek

Or even
From that
Of a stream...

For I
Have not made it
To the sea....

At lease
Not yet....

As my journey
Still carries me...
To that
Of the sea...

That I
Shall one day see...

Now that's
Who I Am...

Can't you see...

As the water itself
Runs wild
And free

As it carries me
To that
Of the sea...

Written by
Ralph L Butler Jr
Rowdy

Who are the
Patriot Guard Riders...
And where
Do they come from...
For it started
Right here
in Oklahoma
in 2005
By a man called
(Twister)

The PGR
is just a group of people
like you and me
Its a person
that will stand
and hold a flag line
at a service
When he or she
is needed
to honor
a fallen soldier

The PGR
is that of person
that will travel
in the rain
and sleet
or even snow
Just to honor
A fellow vet
As he pays
his respect

The PGR
Is a person
That will pray to God
To keep him safe
In his travels
And to give him strength
so that he
can make there in time

To pay his respects
As he himself
Will stand a flag line
for a hero....
That is another
fallen vet...

The PGR
is a group of people
Coming together as one
in a small town
To pay there respects

The PGR
is that of a person
that is humbled
when a member
of the color guard
comes to shake his hand
for standing there
all alone
but he tells them
that there will be more
tomorrow...

The PGR
is that of person
That will spend
many hours
in a flag line
in the cold
of the winter
and even
in the heat
of the summer
only later to find out
that the son
of the man
standing next to you
had committed suicide
after returning
from Iraq

The PGR
is that of the person
Like a parent
or Grandparent
A family member
or even a friend
That has a love one
that is still serving
In the war
over seas

The PGR
is that of person
that maybe a vet
from Viet Nam that was spit on
when they came back
or even
From the gulf wars

The PGR
is that of a person
that will ride his bike
in that of the rain
that he himself
can barely see
as he rides only
by the taillights
from that of those
that are ahead of him
all because
he heard
that some protestors
will be there
at the funeral
of a PFC
or a Sgt
A Captain
or even a Major
or Colonel
Who ever
it way be
As he stands to protect

the family
as he himself
considers it to be
one of the proudest days
of his life
When he sees
over a hundred riders
standing there
When he arrives

The PGR
is that of the person
who could not think
of any other place to be
On that
of the 11th hour
of the 11th day
of the 11th month
as he stands
to honor
A family member
Like his father
His uncle
His brother
His son
Or even that
of a friend
That he had lost
from Viet Nam
Or even
from the persian gulf
As he himself
has received
a Silver Star
two Bronze Stars
and even
a Purple Heart from Desert Storm
to Operation Enduring Freedom
Because he acted
like a soldier
above and beyond
the call of duty

For thats
what they say
About him
But now
He is a father
to many
and his family
had no idea
what he had done

To earn the medals
And the ribbons
that they call
service awards
that he
wanted nothing to do with
Because the military
Had turned there backs on them
And said
You are
an expendable item
because you
grew up
in foster homes
And thats
where it should end
But then
it all
started to make sense
To my family
From the restless nights
tossing and turning
Waking up
Sweating
with tears
For then
it all made sense
Why he wanted
to be a part
of this
the PGR

So remember
A person
that is a vet
Will always
have great honor
pride
and respect
And it will be
that of my honor
to stand with you
when the time is near
as we gather around
But remember
if you ask me
How many
Will there be
from the PGR
that will show up
And all I will say
It might be 100
or even more
For I do not know
but I will
tell you this
I will guarantee you
at lease one...

So being a PGR member
is not fun
it may be
the hardest thing
that you
will ever do
You may have the Mother
of a fallen soldier
cry on your shoulder
thanking you
for being there
And you
might have a Marine
who has escorted
his brother home

from Afghanistan as he stands at
attention
and salutes you
with tears
streaming down his face
As I myself
Will break
and do the same
For I
could not
Hold back...
The way I felt
On that day

So being a member
of the PGR
may not be fun
but you will never
stand with better people
and it may be
one of the most
rewarding things
that you
have ever done
and without a doubt
it will change
your life forever
Like an escort
of a KIA
from Oklahoma City
to Shawnee
Or even the return
Of the dog tags
to a mother...
That lost her son
In Viet Nam
It will touch your heart
In so many ways
As I
am a vet....
And I still see things
from that of my past

That seems
to never pass...
For I'm just one
of many
Of the PGR...

And that
is who we are...

SSGT RALPH LEE BUTLER, JR.

A HIDDEN WORD

Within the words
That are written
There is always
A hidden word
That will come to mind
Which will lead to a sentence
That is all mine
With only one conclusion
To an answer
And a question
That comes together
In my mind
All from a hidden word
In which I'll find
When I come to read
Something
What is written...

Your labor
of today
Is your wealth
of tomorrow

A child's hug
Can make all the difference
When he or she
Can give
Or receive
Even as the child
Still believes...
In that
Of there dreams...

JUST ONE ANGEL

You know
He could of sent
Ten thousand angels
Just to protect me
But really
All I need
Is just one...
As he still
Protects me...

A dream and a pen
go well together
when you write the words
of that of your dream...

A hero once said
For I am not
A hero
Not until the day
That I take
my last breath
For then
You can call me
a hero
As you wish
When the ribbons
and the medals
are laid upon my chest...
As they bury me
With the others
That came here
only to rest...

Dreams from inside
And the sympathy
Of mankind
Will bring us all together
As we give hope
To one another
All
In due time...

For the tragedies
In ones life
Brings out the strength
In that of others
And that my friend
Is the reason why
We all come together
At the very end...

If you talk
with a forked tongue
Then the words you speak
can not be trusted...

Its ok to dream
For it gives you hope
But when it comes
to reality
Then
it is not a dream
Anymore...
For it is something
That is so real
And so very true...
Because you
Have reached something
That is more
Than just a dream...
Anymore...

Let him
And that of no others
Pick the path
That you should travel
As you fallow its journey
To that of your own...
That only you
Shall ever truly know
When it begins
And when it ends
For it is
Your own journey...
As you travel the path
To that of your dreams
That begins
And ends
Only
In that of your journey....

Memories
Are a thing
From the past
That never seem
To ever pass
For its like
A story book
With only the pictures
That only I
shall ever see
As the words themselves
Are just hidden
And tucked away
Deep within my heart
For some are good
And some are not
But once again
It has made me
Who I am
For I can not change
The things
From the past...
But at least
I can try
to change the future
That is at hand
All from that
of my past
But yet
they will still remain
In the pages
Of my book
Not of fiction
But of fact...
So tell me
once again
About the memories
That you have
All from that
of my past...
So that I learn
Just a little more

About the stories
That I have heard
As I try
to figure out
Who I am...
All from the memories
Of the past
As I write
Another chapter
To that
of my past...
That seems
to never come
to an end...
As I try
To figure out
Who
I really am...

Poetry
Is a form of art
Made with words
Which are far
And few between
And no one can fathom
What the writer writes
Except the writer himself
But we can still
come up with
Our own conclusion
To the words
That are written
As we read it again
With a different conclusion
From the simple words
That he has written
In a form
that they call
free poetry
Which is still
A form of art
As we draw a picture
That only we
can now fathom
All from the words
That have been written
That only he
Will ever fathom...

The Meaning
Of A Flag Draped Coffin
Will Always Run Deep
In That Of Our Hearts
As We Remember Those
That We Have Lost...
So Rest In Peace
My Dear Brother
Rest In Peace
My Dear Friend....
As The Life Of A Soldier
Comes To An End...

THERE'S A LESSON IN THE WORDS THAT WE READ AND THAT OF WHICH WE SPEAK

From the words
of wisdom
Will come the words
of knowledge
That we speak
As we listen
To those words
That comes
from our hearts
And that
of our minds
As we try to learn
from that
of a lesson
Of many words
That we read
and even
as we speak...
For they are true
to one another
From the wisdom
To the knowledge
That comes together
as one
Whenever
we speak...

The blade of your tongue

We all got to remember
No matter how sharp
A knife can be
It can still cut
The flesh
Of the human being
As the heart itself
Tries to mend
The open wounds
Once again
From a knife
That seems to cut
The human soul
Just like the words
That are spoken
With a forked tongue...
As it cuts the soul
And makes it bleed
With sorrow
And with pain
That will last
A life time...
So don't you see
That the tongue itself
Is much sharper
Than any blade As it cuts away
What is left
In that
of a human being...

Writing the words
Is just one thing
But living them
Is another thing...

SSGT RALPH LEE BUTLER, JR.

A PIRATES COVE

By the darkness
of the night
I shall hide
like the moon
In the middle
of the night
That is hidden
in the clouds
As I sit anchored
out at sea
For I too shall hide
In the banks
of the shore
In that of the fog
That no others
Shall see
As we all shall rest
In peace
Before it is time
to strike
But at the reckon
Of me first light
We my lad
shall stand up
and fight
For what is ours
And what is right
As we fly our flag
Of that
of the black night

A young boy
Once asked his father
Why are they fighting
And what is that big long bag
And his father said
As he took a deep breath
They are fighting for us today
So that we can live here tomorrow
And for the bag you see
Well son
That's the price
For our freedom today....
And his son said
One day
I will fight like them
And I hope and pray
That I'm not the one
In that bag
But if I am dad
It's ok....
As the little boy stood up
And said
Semper-Fi
And walked away

A young mother
Looked down at her son
Who was dying
Of leukemia
Even though
Her heart
was filled with sadness
She still
had a strong will
For her son
For she wanted him
to grow up
and to fulfill
all of his little dreams
But now it seemed
So impossible
Because the leukemia
Has took its toll
and it would see
to just that
But she still wanted
her son's dreams
to come true
So she took her son's hand
and asked him
have you ever
thought about
what you wanted to be
when you grew up
Or have you ever dreamed
Of something
That you wanted to be
and have you ever wished
Upon a star
for something
in your life
That you wanted to do
And then he said
Mommy
I always wanted
to be a fireman
when I grow up

And she smiled
at her son
and said
Let me see
Just let me see
What I can do
if I can make
your dream come true
As tears fell
From her eyes
And later that day
she went down
to her local fire department
in her home town
Where she met
with the Fire Chief
From all around
who seemed to have
a simple heart
that was made of gold
As she explained
About her son's
final dream
and asked
if it was possible
to give her son
just a simple ride
on a fire truck
And the Chief smiled
and said
Look here my dear
we can do
so much better
than just that
If you'll have him ready
at seven o'clock
On Wednesday morning
then we'll make him
an honorary fireman
for the whole day
For he can come down
to the fire station

SSGT RALPH LEE BUTLER, JR.

And spend the day
he can eat with us
and go out
on all the calls
As he may wish
for the whole nine yards
If he may wish
And if
you'll give us
his sizes
then we will get him
a real
fireman's uniform
with a real fireman's hat
and not
the toy one
that you see
with the real emblem
of our Fire Department
And his very own shield
and a yellow slicker
Just like we wear
with the rubber boots
That are all made
right here
in our home town
so we
can get them ordered
and made
just for him
By Wednesday morning
When I come
To pick him up
And sure enough
three days later
the Fire Chief
picked him up
and got him ready
and all dressed up
in his very own
fireman's uniform
and escorted him

from his hospital bed
to the fire truck
down below
for he got to sit
in the very back
of the ladder truck
as he helped
steer it back
to the fire station
For he
was in hog heaven
on that very day
For there were only
just three calls
And he went out
on them all
on this very day
and he got to ride
in three different trucks
and even
In the Fire Chief's car
He was also videotaped
in the local news
for being
the youngest fireman
in the whole wide world
That made
National news
while having his dream
come true
with all the love
and the support
that just grew
And it seemed to help him
As he lived
three months longer
than any doctor
thought possible
But then
one night
all of his vitals
began to drop

And started shutting down
Just like that
so the head nurse
who believed
that no one
should ever die alone
began calling
family members
one by one
telling them
to come to the hospital
For it was time
And then she remembered
that very day
That he spent
as a fireman
so she called
the Fire Chief
and asked
if it was possible
to send a fireman
to the hospital
to be with him
and the chief replied
We can do better
than just that
for we will be there
in just five minutes
So will you please
do me a favor
When you hear
the sirens screaming
and see the lights
flashing
In the night
will you announce
over the PA
that there is not a fire
It's just the fire department
coming to see
one of its finest members
That came to be

For one last time
before he goes
And will you please
open the window
to his room
And sure enough
about five minutes later
a ladder truck arrived
at the hospital
extending its ladder
right up to his room
and over a dozen
Of firefighters
climbed right on up
into his room
And with
his mother's permission
they hugged him
and held him tight
as they told him
how much they loved him
And with his dying breath
He looked up
at the Chief
and said
Chief
am I really a fireman now
And the Chief replied
With tears in his eyes
Yes sir
You sure are
Your one of the best
A real fireman
That everyone will remember
For years to come
Because you are
a little fighter
And you are
our little hero
From our own town...
And with those words
The little boy smiled

228

All once more
as he closed his eyes
for the very
last time...

AS WATER RUNS FREE
IT WILL ONE DAY FALL
FROM THAT OF A RIVER
OR A STREAM
AS IT NEVER LOOKS BACK
TO THAT OF THE FALL
BECAUSE THE WATER ITSELF
SEEMS TO FLOW
AS IT RUNS WILD AND FREE...
WITH THAT
OF THE ITS FLOW...
SO CAN'T YOU SEE
THAT YOU CAN NEVER
HOLD IT BACK
AS IT TRAVELS
FROM ONE PLACE
TO ANOTHER...
FROM THAT OF ITS FLOW...
AS IT MOVES IN A DIRECTION
THAT IS TRULY
OF ITS OWN...

For this nation
I will take a stand
With liberty
And justice
Because
The constitution
Says I can....
And for my oath
That I took
Simply says
I will
Defend The Constitution
Of The United States
Against all enemies
foreign and domestic
That I
Will bear true faith
And allegiance
To the same
That I
Take this obligation
Freely
So help me God....

The Wings I Bare
Of True Faith
With Allegiance
To The Same

For these
Are the true colors
That will always fly
In the sky
Above me
And when it's time
Go ahead
And cover me
With the same colors
That I defend
As I come to rest
With those very colors
That are now
Draped over me
In remembrance
Of our freedom
That we have
As I served
To protect
That God given right
That he himself
Has given me
With these
Very colors
That still remains
Above me...
As I now
Take flight
With the angels
That surround me...

Under the cover
Of the midnight skies
Comes the words
From a simple stranger
That must of heard
My every prayer
As I listen
To those hidden words
That touches
The hearts and souls
Of so many
When we truly
Need them most
So tell me
Oh Lord
Was it truly
Just a stranger
That came to me
From the middle
Of nowhere
Or was it an Angel
With the words
So soft and dear
That was sent here
Just for me
Out of the mist
Of nowhere
With the words
That only he
Would ever say
That I remember
From back in the day
For I know
Without a doubt
That he still watches
Over me...
From the silence
Of a whisper
With those very words
That are meant
Only for me
As I hear him say

Reach for the stars
My son
Reach for the stars
And heal thy self
As it will come to be
Because you are
A shining star
That will always be
In my book
Don't you see
As you teach others
To reach for the stars
Just like
You and me
But always remember
Heal thy self
And you will see
As it comes to past
As you help others
From the words
Of your past...

For the tears
That we have shed
Through out the years...
We can not count
From the strangers
That we have meet...
All because
Of a tragedy
That took place
Somewhere
Along a road
Or highway
That we still remember
As we pass on by
With only that
But a tear
All once more
As we remember
Him
or Her
And even
That child
That we had lost
As we held their hands
Somewhere
Out here.....
But some of you
Will only see
The remains
Of a Cross....
That still
Lays here....
To remember those
That we had lost....
From that
Of the past

Written by
Ralph L Butler Jr
Rowdy

A ghost of your past
Will always whisper
Even in the silence
of the winds
As the storm may pass
With nothing to see
Except only
The memories
Of your past...

Let the boots of my journey
Be filled with the treasures
That the heart and soul
Will ever need
As they are filled
With the love
And the support
From other firefighters
Like me
To that
Of the 19
The hotshots
That will always be...
In the company
Of our dreams
As the angels from heaven
Kneel next to me...

The flames will always burn
In the background
Of those skies
As the hearts will bleed
And the tears will fall
From that of the memories
Of our past
But please
Remember this
From the heat
And the flames
That we have fought
For such a long time
Will always run deep
In that of our veins
As we live
For the sound
Of that alarm
Just one more time
Before
They lay me to rest
So let me hear it
All once more
As you all
Gather around
To the last call
Of the 19
As we come here
To rest
From a battle
Like no other
But still yet
Our memories
And our actions
Will always live on
As they lay me here
In the green grass
Where my boots
And my shield
Now comes
To a rest
Right here

Beside me
As the angels from heaven
Now lead me home
On this last call...
Through the flames of glory
That runs deep
In our souls....
For we are now
Heaven bound
On a latter
Made of gold
As the angels
Lead us home
And you my brother
Will never
Stand alone....

What lays here
From the fire and flames
As the smoke disappears
You will see
What is left
In the memories
Of the ashes
That you now see
But soon
And soon enough
You will see
The green grass
Of the 19
As we rest
Where no flames
Will ever burn
For we
Are the 19
The Hotshots
Of Granite Mountain
That you
Will come to know
and see
As we live on
In a legacy
Of many firefighters
That came
Before me....
So out of the ashes
We will rise
All once more
Into a legacy
Of the 19

In this chain
Holds a link
Like no other
For this is our strength
To one another
Because
Each and every one
Holds us together
Like that
Of no other
But now
There is just one
That holds the key
To this bond
That will last
Forever
As you my brother
Will keep us all
Together
And you yourself
Must carry on
With the dreams
Of each other
To the 19
Plus one
That still holds
Us together
The Hotshots
Of Granite Mountain
Forever...

A DREAM

FOR THE DREAM
I DREAM
IS A DREAM
NOT SEEN

BECAUSE
I CAN ONLY DREAM
A DREAM FOR ME

SO
IN THIS DREAM
I WILL DREAM
A DREAM FOR ME

EVEN THOUGH
I WANT MORE
THAN JUST A DREAM

IT WILL ALWAYS BE
AND REMAIN
A DREAM
AN ENTER DREAM
FOR ME

ONLY IN THE EYES
OF MY DAUGHTER

From a moment of memory
In that of time
With my daughter
When I stood right there
Beside her...
When she
Needed me most
As I can remember
That very day...
When her hair
Was up in a pony tail
And she was wearing
Her favorite little blue dress
Tied with a yellow a bow
For today
was the day
that they had called
Daddy's Day
That all
would get to know
When we
Would come together
At her school
And she just
Couldn't wait
To get to school
On this very day
But her mommy tried
To tell her why
That she just
Should not go
For she wanted her
To just stay at home
Because the kids themselves
Might not understand
Just why
She would come to school
All alone
Without her daddy

By her side
On such
A very special day
But she was not afraid
In any way
For she knew
In her heart
Just what to say
And even
What to do
As she told her class
Just why
He wasn't there
On Daddy's Day
But still
Her mother worried
Because she knew
Deep down inside
That her daughter
Would have to face
This very day
One day soon
But she just
Didn't want her
To face it
All on her own
And that was why
She had tried
To keep her daughter
All at home
But long
And behold
The little girl
Was so determined
To go school
Anyway
So eager and willing
To tell them all
About her daddy
That she never sees
And that never calls
For there were daddies

All along the wall
In the back of her room
That everyone could see
But soon
And soon enough
They would all
Get to meet
As the children themselves
Where squirming around
So impatiently
In that of their seats
So one by one
The teacher called
A student up
In front of the class
Just to introduce their daddy
As time itself
Began to slowly pass
And now at last
The teacher called
Her little name
And every child
In that room
Turned there heads
And began to stare
Each of them was searching
For such a man
That wasn't their
Where's your daddy
She heard
a young boy shout out
And then she heard
Another one say
In a hateful way
She probably doesn't have one
That a child
Would dare to shout
And from somewhere
In the back of the room
She heard
someones daddy
simply say

SSGT RALPH LEE BUTLER, JR.

Seems to me
He must be
Just another deadbeat daddy
Thats just too busy
To spend his day
With his own daughter
On this very day
But the words themselves
Did not offend her
In any way
For she began to smiled
When she looked up
As she saw her Mommy
Standing right their
And then
She looked back
At her teacher
Who just told her
To just go on
And with her hands
Behind her back
She began to speak
Just like that
And out of the mouth
Of this very child
Came the words
That was so incredible
And so very unique
And yet
so very proud
When she said
My Daddy
Could not be here
Because he lives
so far away
But I know
Without a doubt
That he wishes
That he could be right here
with me today
Since this is
My daddy's day

And though
You can not meet him
I wanted you all
Just to know
About my daddy
That's so big
And tall
For he's so brave
That he gave his all
To this country
For you and me
All because
He loves us so
For he used to tell me stories
And he taught me
to ride my bike
He surprised me
Many times
with just
a single yellow rose
That he would leave behind
And he always said
that the yellow rose
Is only fit
for a hidden angel
And that one day
It will turn
to a golden rose
In just
a blink of an eye
And he even taught me
to fly a kite
And we used to share
our hot fudge sundaes
and even
our ice cream cones
And though
You can not see him
I want you all
just to know
That I'm standing here
But really

not alone
For he is always with me
Even though it seems
That he is
so far away
But I still know
That he is real close
Because the flag
Up on the pole
Tells me so
As he waves back
At mommy and me
From each and every pole
That I come to see
And then
she took her right hand
And laid it on her chest
Feeling her little heartbeat
Beneath her favorite
little blue dress
And somewhere
From among the crowd
Of those daddy's
Stood a mother
That was so proud
Even though
She was lost in tears
Watching
her baby girl
That wasn't a baby
anymore
For she was so brave
And beyond her years
As she stood up
For the love of a man
That is not
in her life at all
And then
she dropped her little hand
Back down to her side
Staring straight ahead
Into this very crowd

As she finished
With a voice
That was so soft
And so proud
For the message itself
Was loud and clear
As she said it again
all once more
I love my daddy
So very much
For he's my hero
like a shinning star
That seems to shine
each and every night
And if he could
He would be
right here
But heaven itself
Is just too far
So you see
He's so much more
than just my daddy
Don't you see
For he
Was a Soldier
That had died
For you and me
This past year
When an RPG
Hit his humvee
And took his life
Just like that
In the blink of an eye
But sometimes
When I close my eyes
I still see
my daddy
Standing here
For it's like
He never left
and never
went away

SSGT RALPH LEE BUTLER, JR.

And then
she closed her little blue eyes
As she saw him their
All once more
On this very day
And at her mother's surprise
She witnessed something
Of a miracle
That had made her cry
All because
she saw a room
Full of strangers
filled with daddy's
And children
All starting
To close their eyes
For who knows
What they saw
On this very day
And who really knows
What they felt
Deep inside
Perhaps
For merely
Just a second
or even two
in that moment of time
That they might of seen
a soldier
In his dress blues
Standing right their
by her side
As she whispered out loud
I know you're with me Daddy
I know your here
All in the silence
of that room
And what happened next
Made believers
Out of them all
For no one in that room
Would be able to explain

what had happen
On this very day
Because each
and every eye
had been closed
But there
on that very desk
beside the little girl
was a such
a beautiful site
That no one
Would ever
be able to explain
Was a single yellow rose
That had turned
To a golden rose
with the leaves
Of a red fern
That no one
Had ever seen before
For this was truly
A gift for a child
that has been blessed
for just a moment
in that of time
That would last
A life time
All from the love
of a soldier
that was her dad
That only he
Would of left behind
For his daughter
That he calls
His little angel
That now believes
that heaven itself
is never to far
Because daddy's
And soldiers
Are always right here
Holding their daughters

little hands
And I for one
will always be
Right here
In the moment of need
So all you got to do
Is just close
your pretty little eyes...
And just believe...
Because the hidden soldier
Behind those eyes
Will always be
Your daddy...
Can't you see
But only
In the eyes
Of my daughter...

JUST A DIME

A long time ago
a poor young boy
was selling stuff
from door to door

Just trying
to pay his way
through school

For he had nothing
but only a dime
to his name

He was very hungry
So he though to himself
I will ask
for a meal
at the very next house

But
he lost his nerve
when a young woman
opened the door

Instead of asking
for a meal
He just asked
for a drink of water
instead

After seeing him there
She thought to herself
he might be hungry

So she brought him
a glass of milk
and a peanut butter sandwich

To his delight
he drank the milk

and he enjoyed the sandwich
and her company as well.

For he felt like a king

Then he asked her
How much
do I owe you
For I only
got a dime

Is that all you got
she said
and giggled
with a beautiful smile

Then she said:

"You don't owe me anything,"

For the lord has taught me,
to never accept
any kind of payment
for an act of kindness
For this
is what he
would have done

Then he said
Thank you
Thank you from the bottom
of my heart
for such a beautiful meal
and making me feel like a king

Then she said
Let me trade you
for that dime

For this envelope
has a little cash
of mine

and I really
want to trade you
for that dime

and
as they did

She was able
to sneak that dime
into the envelope

And for money
that was in the envelope
it was enough for him
to go to school

For he could not open it
until the next day

For this
was her request
Because
She was going away

So he told her
once more
I will never
forget this day
and I will always
remember you
and your act of kindness

For I feel
so much stronger,
mentally and physically too

But it seemed
as if
I was giving up
on the faith that I had

Until
We sat together
side by side
and you read to me
this scripture
(Isaiah 40: 28-31)

28 Do you not know?
Have you not heard?
The LORD is the everlasting God,
the Creator of the ends of the earth.
He will not grow tired or weary,
and his understanding no one can
fathom.

29 He gives strength to the weary
and increases the power of the weak.

30 Even youths grow tired and weary,
and young men stumble and fall;

31 but those who hope in the LORD
will renew their strength.
They will soar on wings like eagles;
they will run and not grow weary,
they will walk and not be faint.

WELL:
Many years later
That same young woman
became critically ill.

The local doctors
were lost
and could not
find a cure

So they sent her
out of state
To a bigger hospital

Where they

could call upon
the best of the best

So some doctor could study
such a rare disease

So when the doctor came
to the hospital
he was able to heard more
about her illness
and her disease

So now
it was up to him
just to see
what he might
be able to do

But
when he heard her name
and the town
that she came from

A strange feeling
came over him
As tears filled his eyes

So he got up
and went to her room

That's
when he realized
that it was her

He went back
to the meeting room

Flat determined
to do his best
Just to save her life

So from that day on

He dedicated himself
all to her

For he treated her
as if she was a Queen

But after
a long, long struggle
The battle
was finally won

So the doctor requested
That the final bill
be handed to him
for his final approval
and review

So he looked at the bill
and then
he wrote something inside

Then the bill
was sent
to her room

She didn't want to open it
For she knew
It would take
the rest of her life
to pay it off

But finally
she opened it up
and something
caught her eye

Attached to the bill
was a dime

Then she read those words ...

"This bill is paid in full"

Because
Of a glass of milk
and a peanut butter sandwich
with a scripture or two
and the trade
of a dime

So now
I can give back to you
your dime

and so she read on

DO UNTO OTHERS
AS YOU WANT OTHERS
TO DO UNTO YOU

For this is from
Matthew 7:12

Tears of joy
poured from her eyes
as she began to pray

Saying:

"Thank You Dear Lord,
Thank You
for showing me the love
that has spread
through the hearts
and through the hands
of man kind
Thank You God,
Thank You
Amen."

How the times change
As the mind wonders
Like a stream that travels
With the water that moves
Right through your hands
As it falls
From your finger tips
Much like the sand
That moves
Through the hour glass...

I got miles behind me
And miles to go
As I travel
This hard long road
With ups and downs
From all around
But heaven only knows
Where I'm bound

If the grass
Is always greener
On the other side
Then tell me why
You want to come back
To this side...
As you come to graze
Somewhere
On the other side
Of a barb wire fence
That seems
To separate
You and I
That we ourselves
Will never build
Or even support
As you travel
Back and forth
Down this road
As you will find
That the grass itself
Is always greener
Right here
Than the day before
As you drift away
And begin to walk
Down another path
To some ole road
That will lead you
To the middle
Of nowhere
As you try to find
Your way back
To the green grass
That still grows
Right here
Just like
The day before...

It has come
But just once
in a life time
For many of years
When the sky itself
Turns as bright
as the sun
Deep in the mist
of a winters night
That they
have come to call
The red moon
As it lays naked
Deep in the valleys below
Where the streams
Run wild and free
As they sparkle
Like gold
Shifting
in a pan
That lays only
In your hands
Where the dreams themselves
Come to life
Somewhere
In the depth
Of the middle of the night....
For it only comes
But just once
In a life time
If it ever
comes at all
Threw the night
That they call
The red moon
As the sparrow flys
Like the eagle above
In the morning sky's
Where the mouse will rest
Deep in the den
With the grizzle bear
Side by side

Where the spirits
Of them all
Become
Just one
As it happens
Only once
In a life time...
As the spirit
of the moon
Finds its voice
Deep in the shadows
Of its own
Silhouette...

How can you
do something
like this...
When it truly hurts someone
That you do not know
Or even understand
Unless
you have a forked tongue...
Like a hand shake
in one hand
and a knife
in the other...
As you say
Welcome
and or hello
To someone
That you call
a brother
or a friend...
But only
in front of them
And in the presence
of others
That stand
around him
But
As you walk away
And say
something
A whole lot different
to your group
that is a click
from within
As you down grade
One of your own...
So tell me again
What ever happen
to the phrase:
Brothers forever
And Brothers
for life....
For brothers in arms...

You are not forgotten....
And no one
is left behind....
So united
We shall stand
And divided
We shall fall
So think about it again
Before you say
Or do anything
at all
Because
we all come
from different
walks of life
And remember this
That you have to
like yourself
Before you can ever
like someone else....
And this
can only be said
From someone
That has been treated
Just like this
as you delete them
And leave them
Behind
Just for your own power
And you greed
With nothing
But a political gain....

My pencil
And my pen
Will always
Make a point
From the words
That I write
But if you choose
To take them away
Well then
The words will be written
In the blood
That I have shed
From the past
To the present
As the words are written
From my own hands...

Character

Never be ashamed
Of the scars
That you have
For it shows a character
In where you've been
And it really shows
The strength
That you have
In your life
As you carry on
So hold your head up
And say out loud
I can
And I will
Survive
Even as the scars
Still live
Deep inside
As I carry on
With my life

I have seen
many children
Strive to overcome
many things
In their lives
As they learn
To overcome
The horizon
of the moon
Into a path
Which will become
One of their own
Much like a journey
That seems
To never end
As they strive
All over again
From place to place
And from home to home
As they learn to adapt
As they travel
Back and forth
But with really
Nowhere to go
And no place
To really call home
As they travel
All alone
With the hopes of a dream
Of just somewhere
To go...
As they travel
Back and forth
But still
All alone...

Its More Than Just A Word

Words
are just words
But a phrase
of words
Are words
from an expression
That has been written
All because
of a signal word
That needs
an expression
As it is written

ITS NOTHING
BUT AN ADVENTURE
FROM THE TRAVELS
IN YOUR DREAMS

I can travel by land
Or I can travel by sea
But if I travel by air
I will miss
an adventure
of many things
So if I travel by sea
I will see things
That the land
Will never see
But if I travel by land
I will never
truly see
How the sea
Can ever breath
With out me
But still
by land alone
That I seem to travel
most of all
From the hills
And the mountains
That I travel
and see
Shall be
like the waves
Of the ocean
That I travel
Only by sea
But if
I shall travel
by air
I can see everything
That I see
But I will still miss
The adventure

That I truly see
By land
And even
by sea...

Ole' lad
Thrive not
On the blood
Of each other
But thrive
On the will
From each other...
For then you'll learn
A whole lot more
Than what
You've bargained for...
Much like a Scotsman
Fighting
For what is right
And what is his
All from the beginning
of our time
A true
Freedom Fighter
And a Scotsman
To boot....

Sometimes
The things that we regret
Will not come
From that
Of an order....
As we live with them
Each and every day....
With that of the blood
That still remains
On our hands
Even today
That only we
Will ever see
With a hidden tear
That only falls
In that of the shadows
Of our dreams
But only
When I am alone
So that no one else
Will ever see...
From the pain
That is still hidden
And tucked away
From the memories
Of yesterday....

THE HIDDEN SPIRIT
FROM WITHIN

If We
Could Only See
The True Spirit
That Is In
One Another
Just Imagine
What We Can Learn
From One Another
If We
Could Only See
The True Spirit
That Is Hidden
In One Another

Written by
Ralph L Butler Hr
Rowdy

The voice of the man
Can say many things
With a tone
Of a different sound
But if you listen
To his words
Then you will find
Something different
About that sound
As the words are hidden
In his voice
With a different sound
Because his eyes
Will say it all
If you would only listen
To the sounds....

The marks of a wound

Just because
A wound on the outside
Appears to be healed
Doesn't mean
It is healed on the inside...
As it carries that of a scar
That are really
Too deep to mend
As they are easily
Ripped open again..

The soul of a man
Is hidden
By his enter spirit
But if he
Shall ever
Set it free
Then he will see
Whatever
The heart may hold
As the pain
and tears
Are set free
Until
He holds back
What he
Is afraid to see
Whatever
It may be
From his past
That he
Doesn't want
Others to see
For it is hidden
In the spirit
Of his soul...

MY FRIEND

WHEN I WAS
JUST A BABY
I HEARD ABOUT
A MAN NAMED JESUS

WHEN I BECAME
A CHILD
WE USE TO PLAY
GAMES TOGETHER

AND WHEN I BECAME
A TEEN
I TURNED MY BACK
ON HIM

AND WHEN I BECAME
A MAN
I FOUND
HIM AGAIN

AND THIS IS WHAT
HE SAID
WHERE HAVE YOU
BEEN MY FRIEND

WHEN YOU WERE
JUST A BABY
YOU HEARD
MY NAME

AND WHEN YOU WERE
A CHILD
WE USE TO SIT
AND TALK A WHILE

AND WHEN YOU WERE
A TEEN
I TRIED TO GUIDE YOU
AND CARRY YOU ALONG
THE WAY

SSGT RALPH LEE BUTLER, JR.

AND NOW THAT YOUR
A MAN
YOU HAVE CALLED
MY NAME

SO WE WILL TALK
AND I WILL
GUIDE YOU
AND CARRY YOU
JUST AS I HAVE BEFORE
MY FRIEND

Let the sun settle
to the west
As she rises
From the east
For there is beauty
In the sunrise
And there is beauty
In the sunset
As she comes to rest
But still yet
Her light will shine
In the darkness
Of the night
As it reflects
From the moon
In the middle of the night
For its her beauty
That still shines
Throughout the day
And into the night

Journey

Live for the journey
And not
For the results
And the benefits
Of the journey
For then
You will know
That you
Have lived a life
Within a journey
To that which is
A journey of life
For there is
No beginning
And there is
No end
Because
It's just that
A journey
A journey
With no end....
And a journey
To no end....
Because life itself
Is that
Of a journey

What do you see
When you come to see
What many
Do not see...

Its the heart and soul
Of yourself
Is what
You'll come to see

We are all teachers
And we are still students
At the same time...
So listen
As they speak
And you will learn
Something
That is very unique
That will help you
Make a difference
In someone's life
When you speak
And teach
Something
That is just as unique
Not only
As a teacher
But as a student
As well...
As we all come together
In a classroom
No greater
Than the other
With the words
That are now
So unique
When a teacher
And a student
Become one of the same
Like that
of no other
As we learn
And teach
With the words
That are so unique

The west was won
By the hand of a gun
When mankind
Stood for the law
And the law of the land...
For that's
Where law and order
All began
With a Bible
In the other hand...

Your heart is free
Now take the courage
And follow it
To wherever
It may be...

WHEN
GREAT MINDS
THINK ALIKE

WE CAN CREATE
AND ACCOMPLISH
MANY THINGS
IN OUR LIVES

AS WE OVERCOME
AND ADAPT
TO THE OBSTACLES
THAT ARE IN
OUR LIVES

SO
IF WE WOULD ONLY
WORK TOGETHER

THINK ABOUT
THE THINGS
THAT WE CAN DO

WITHOUT THE FEAR
OF BEING HURT
OR SAYING
SOMETHING WRONG

AND JUST BECAUSE
WE DO NOT UNDERSTAND
THE THINGS YOU SAY
OR EVEN DO

IT DOES NOT MEAN
THAT WE ARE WEAK

BECAUSE
WE ARE TRUELY
STRONGER
THAN YOU WILL EVER KNOW

SO WE CAN
AND WE WILL
OVERCOME
AND ADAPT
TO THE OBSTACLES
THAT ARE IN OUR LIVES

WITH OUT ANY BOUNDARIES
TO HOLD US BACK

AS WE COME TOGETHER
LIKE SO MANY HAVE DONE
IN THE PAST

FOR NO ONE
SHOULD EVER BE
LEFT BEHIND
OR EVEN FELT
LIKE THEY HAVE

JUST BECAUSE
OF YOUR LACK
IN LEADERSHIP

OR BECAUSE
OF THE WEAKNESS
THAT IS IN YOUR LEADERSHIP
THAT WILL CAUSE
MANY TO FALL

AS WE HAVE SEEN
SO MANY TIMES BEFORE

AND THE WEAKNESS
THAT SEEMS TO FALL
WILL HAVE COME FROM YOUR
GUIDANCE
THAT YOU HAVE GIVEN
TO US ALL

SO
IF WE WOULD ONLY
COME TOGETHER
AS GREAT MINDS
ARE KNOWN TO DO

THEN
WE CAN
AND WE WILL
HAVE A BETTER LEADERSHIP
IN WHAT YOU DO

BECAUSE
WE CAN ALL
BE LEADERS
AS WE HELP THOSE
WHO DO NOT KNOW

AND THAT
IS WHAT TRUE LEADERS
WILL ALWAYS DO

SO LET US SEE
WHAT KIND OF LEADERSHIP
THAT YOU
MIGHT DO

BECAUSE LEADERS
WILL LEAD
WITH THE STRENGTH
OF THE UNKNOWN

WHEN
GREAT MINDS
COME TOGETHER
AND THINK
SO MUCH ALIKE
WHEN WE DO

POETIC JUSTICE

POETIC JUSTICE
STRIKES AGAIN !!
WITH A RED-NECK VERB
BEHIND IT !!

ALL BECAUSE I FILED FOR A
LICENSE, WITH THE UNITED
STATES SUPREME COURT

SO NOW
I AM ABLE
TO WRITE AND TO SPELL
MY OWN WORDS

FOR I CAN NOT SAY

FOR I KNOW NOT
WHAT I WRITE
BUT I KNOW
WHAT I MEAN

BUT NOW
I CAN SAY

I KNOW NOW
WHAT I WRITE
AND WHAT I MEAN

BECAUSE
I KNOW
E-V-E-R-Y-T-H-I-N-G

POETIC JUSTICE
STRIKES AGAIN !!
WITH A RED-NECK VERB
BEHIND IT !!

Remember your freedom
For its only
What you make it
As you spread your wings
And begin
To fly away....
As the sun sets
For another day...
And no one
Really knows
What tomorrow holds
As we remember
The flight we took
Throughout the day
As it ends
In the dusk
Of the evening skies
With only a dream
Of another day
As we begin
All over again
When we take flight
To the morning skies
As life itself
Comes alive
In the beauty
Of the morning skies
With only the freedom
Of today

The badge
Or the shield
Does not protect me
But the weapon in my hand
Sure does...
As I protect
This here land
That I am on...
For this is my freedom
That is at hand
As I take a stand...
To protect the constitution
Of this great land...
For it is written
In that of stone
All across this land
As we stand to protect
What is left
Of this dying land...
And it is now
What we make it...
As we come together
And take a stand
For what is right
On the foundation
That was built
On this land
With the constitution
And the Bible
In our hands...
But with out them
We have nothing
As the Statue of Liberty
Is shaking her fist
And the Liberty Bell
Sounds no more
For this
Is a sad site to see
With all the signs
That simply says
Our flag
Of the USA

Is now in jeopardy
As she is folded
And tucked away....
So tell me
And show me
Your true colors
Before she
Is taken away....
And can you say
God Bless the USA
Before that too
Is taken away...

Have you ever read a story,
That truly
has no ending...
Then just ask someone
Who they are...
For it is truly
A never ending story....

Let the sun
Cast its shadow
In that
Of what you seek
As you fallow something
That is so very
Unique
As the sun itself
Rises again
To something
That is unique
Deep within
Its own shadows
That only you
Will ever
Come to seek...
As the sun
Comes to rest
In the western skies
As we all
Will come to rest...
From the shadows
That are leaning
Back to the west
When the sun itself
Rises
Once again
In the shadows
That we seek
With out ever
Looking back....

Hold on to your dreams
For they will hold on to you
As they carry you away
To that of another day....

SSGT RALPH LEE BUTLER, JR.

If I drove 1 mile
Then I drove 10
Before I realize
That I got to start
All over again
So with 100 miles behind me
And still yet
A 100 more to go
I will soon
Deliver my load
Wherever it leads me
And wherever
I may go...
Until the day
I pick up
Another load
That's between
A 100 or two...
Or maybe
A whole lot more
Then I want to do
With over
A million miles behind me
That I've scored
Throughout the years
As I add
Just a few more
To that running score
As I travel
The open road
Back and forth
From shore to shore
As I come to rest
In the middle
Of nowhere

Words of wisdom
Comes from the knowledge
And the experience
Of ones past
As we move forward
Into the future
Without ever
Looking back...

The Pride And Honor
<u>Of A Daughter</u>

When she was born
I was so proud
As she fallowed
My foot steps
All around

But then she grew up
A soldier to be
As she took an oath
And once more
I shed a tear
As baby girl
Went off to war

But right then and there
I started to realized
That my baby girl
Is not a baby
Anymore

For she is a soldier
That makes me so proud
As she stands in her boots
All on her own
Just like
I taught her to do

And now
I see her there
Standing tall
And looking good
In that uniform
As she protects this land
Like so many do

But she will always be
And she will always remain
My baby girl...

Just to me
That makes me so proud

So with honor
and with pride
She is still
My baby girl...

And she will stand
In the ranks
Of any man
For this is her pride
And her honor
As she serves
As my daughter

SSGT RALPH LEE BUTLER, JR.

THE HIDDEN PICTUERS

I still have
many pictures
in my heart
And in my mind
that I still see
Over and over again
Each and every day
As the words themselves
Are just hidden
And tucked away
Deep within myself...
But some day
You will see
And read something
Of a view
That will touch your heart
And will never
Go away...
As you yourself
Will tuck it away...

Your eyes will see
Only what you want them to see
And because of this
You will never
Truly see
As you close your eyes
And walk away
But if
You close your eyes
And just listen
Then you will see
More than eyes
Will ever see...

Today's journey
will lead you to tomorrow
but tomorrow still holds
another journey
something
like today....
but still
so much different
in its own way....

My ole Chevy
Runs a little heavy
When she gets alittle
Bogged down
Right down
To the nitty gritty
But let me tell you what
Boys
She'll jump right up
When I crank her up
Slinging that mud
From side to side
Right here
Right now
Mud boggin
Mud doggin
All the way
To the other side
As you take alittle ride
In my ole Chevy
That runs a little heavy
When she gets alittle
Bogged down
Right down
To the nitty gritty
In my ole Chevy
That runs alittle heavy
Yeh ha
Yippee ki yah
Skin em and get em there boys
That yah'll would say
From town to town
When yah'll sing
My ole Chevy
Runs alittle heavy
When she gets alittle
Bogged down
Right down
To the nitty gritty
In my ole Chevy...
That's alittle heavy
When she gets alittle

Bogged down
Right down
To the nitty gritty
Yeh ha
Yippee ki yah
Skin em and get em
As I come to town
In my ole Chevy....

Remember
Life Is a challenge
And we battle it
All the time
But really
What makes it harder
Is when
We fight ourselves
To no end
And don't even
Know why...

I am that journey
In which it falls
For the heart is heavy
And nowhere to roam
As I seek my dreams
In my heart
As I travel
All alone

From the words
that are written
Comes something
That's so unique
That will touch the hearts
Of many
with something...
That seems
So sweet
Other than
Some ole words
That you
Will come to read
As you find the answers
To your question
That you seek
That are only written...
From my heart
As we speak
With the words
That you seek...

I will see you
In the day
And the day after
As the sun sets
And the moon rises
Before tomorrow
Ever comes
As the night shall fall
To the morning sky's
From here on after...
As I wake
Only from my dreams
That only I
Will ever see
As tomorrow comes
And speaks
Only to me
With the last breath
That I
Will ever take
As I speak out
And say
Freedom
Freedom to all
That has ever fought
With the battle scars
Of freedom
That only you
Will ever see
As it comes to me
In that of my dreams
As I close my eyes
With the hidden tears
That seems to fall
From my eyes
As I wake
From those very dreams
Of yesterday

Take the time and read it

Sometimes
You got to read it
To see it...
As you feel the words
From that of your own....

Just a single word
From that of a sentence
Will make you think
About that phrase
Or sentence
As it can be changed
From that of another
To that of your own
From a single word
That you will call
All of your own
But it truly is
Still of the same
Like the phrase itself
When it first became
With only one difference
To that of the change
Of a single word
Because it was different
From that of your own
With a different ending....
From that
Of the start...
Because of one word
That is your own...

Standing in the silence of the wind
With only the sound of our flags
Whispering
In the breeze of the wind
As the eyes will see
What the hearts do breath
From that of the winds
As the silence of those words
Now whisper
In those very winds
So rest in peace
My dear friend
Rest in peace
As the winds
Carries your voice
To that of no end
As you whisper
Into the wind...

Love it's self
Holds no bars
And every year
Is just a day
And every day
Is like
another year
For our love has grown
For the past
10 years or so
But we
have been together
For that of eleven
That seems to me
Like a life time
Living with you
in heaven
But threw the time
That has passed
I can say to you
Without you
I am nothing
As I hear you say
To me
That I
am your best friend
And without each other
We are both lost
Like a boat at sea
With no sails to guide
You and me
But whenever
A storm has hit
We found a way
To fix whatever
It may be
Because our love
It stronger
Than any waves...
As we say
To each other
Happy Anniversary

To 10 years
And then 11
For we are more
than best friends
For we
Are a couple...
To the end...

When does a path
become a trail
or a trail
become a path
much like a road
that becomes a highway
or even
a toll road
after all
is it set
by the foundation
of its builders
of how many people
will travel its path
or even its trail
before it becomes
a country road
so it seems
that the one
that started it all
really
has no say at all
as he walks it
all alone...
from a path
or a trail
to that
of a country road....
that now leads
to my home....

The Hooves Of An Angel

I have come to see
Many of you
Threw the years
As you come and go
Just as you please
But some
Have never come back
As I was born
Right here
Watching over
All of you
From the stones
In the green grass
But now
I am here
But not in flesh
As I roam
In the memories
Of the past
But if
You look close
You will see
My mother
And me
As we cross
And bed down
In the green grass...

A Truckers Life

The road I travel
I've traveled many times
But where I'm going
i still don't know
for its different
every time...
As I travel
Back and forth
From where
i may roam...
but im never
all alone

He gives us direction
But the choices we make
Sometimes makes obstacles
In the directions we travel
But threw him
All things are possible
If we let the lord
Lead the way

A FAMILY TO BE

WHEN YOUR SON
TAKES A WIFE
YOU KNOW NOW
HE HAS A LIFE

A LIFE
THAT HE WILL SHARE
WITH HIS WIFE

SO
WITH THIS MARRIAGE
YOU HAVE MADE US PROUD

BECAUSE
YOUR WIFE
IS NOW
APART OF OUR LIVES

A NEW DAUGHTER
THAT WE CAN CHERISH

AND
HOLD DEAR
TO OUR LIVES

AND
IN THIS MARRIAGE
YOU HAVE GIVEN US
NOT ONE
OR TWO
BUT THREE
MORE GRANDKIDS

TO BRIGHTEN OUR DAYS
JUST LIKE TODAY

SO
REMEMBER THIS DAY
AS YOUR HANDS
ARE JOINED

AND
YOUR HEARTS
ARE ONE

BECAUSE
THE LOVE YOU FOUND
IS JOINED AT LAST

AND
WITH THIS IN MIND
HERE IS OUR HANDS

AND WORDS
FROM OUR HEARTS
SO WE CAN
DRINK
A DRINK

AND TOAST
A TOAST

TO THE BOTTOM
OF THIS GLASS
YOU CAN FINELY
RELAX AT LAST

FOR THIS
IS JUST THE START
OF A NEW BEGINNING
IN OUR FRIENDSHIP
AS WE COME TO TRUST
ONE ANOTHER
LIKE FRIENDS
WILL DO

Written by
Ralph L Butler Jr
Rowdy

Lessons

There's a lesson
In the words
That we read
And that
Of which we speak

From the words
Of wisdom
Will come the words
Of knowledge
That we speak
As we listen
To those words
That comes
From our hearts
And that
Of our minds
As we try to learn
From that
Of a lesson
Of many words
That we read
And even
As we speak...
For they are true
To one another
From the wisdom
To the knowledge
That comes together
As one
Whenever
We speak...

I STILL LIVE

TO LOVE ON EARTH
IS ONLY SHORT LIVED
BUT OUR LOVE IN HEAVEN
WILL ALWAYS LIVE

FOR THE LOVE YOU HAVE
WILL ALWAYS BE
FROM YOUR MOTHER
ON TO YOU

WITH HER CHILDREN AT
HAND
YOUR MOTHER
WILL ALWAYS SHINE THROUGH

SO I SEE IN YOU
THE LOVE SHE HAD
EVEN THOUGH
SHE IS GONE
SHE STILL LIVES
IN ALL OF YOU

SO REMEMBER
THE LOVE YOU HAVE
FOR EACH OTHER
STARTED
WITH YOUR MOTHER

AND BECAUSE OF YOU
SHE WILL ALWAYS LIVE
IN OUR HEARTS
AND IN OUR MINDS
FOREVER

BECAUSE
SHE
STILL LIVES

WRITTEN BY
ROWDY L BUTLER

The sky's the limit
But you can not reach it alone
So build your dreams with someone
And together
You can reach for the stars
As you live your dreams
That you hold on to
When you say
The sky's the limit
And I'm just one
Of many stars...

You are my light
that gives me life
as I stand right here
in the shadow
of the perfect silhouette
that will always reflect
an image
that you will see
whenever
you shine on me...

The Wallace's of Scotland
Will fight to be men
So says the journey
of such a man
That comes from a fight
From deep within
But yet his battle
Comes from his knowledge
From his own hands
With that
of a noble man
For it's truly
his own wits
That will make him
Who he is
When he becomes
Of such a man...
Into a battle
Of no end
From the heritage
That lays within
From the blood
Of his own clan
That is known
By many
As the patriot
A hero
Across this land
As he takes a stand
Once again
For what is ours
And what is not
When they call
Upon his name
So once again
Into a battle
Of freedom
With that of no end...
For they
can take my life
But they will never
Take my freedom

For this
is a promise
Of just one man
As it comes
Only from within....
A legacy
That still lives
In the freedom
Of this land

If I gave you
My today
Would you be willing
To give me
Your tomorrow
As we look forward
To today
As it leads us
To tomorrow
Until the day
They lay me to rest
And it will be
One day soon
But let it not be
Today
Or tomorrow
As our love
Grows together
In one another
As we live
for today
And look forward
To tomorrow
As I give to you
My today
Each
and every day
From this day forward
With love
And understanding
That will last
Forever
When I say....
I do
Just as I did
13 years ago
On August 31 2000
And nothing
has really changed
Except maybe
The strength
And the love

That we have
In one another....
That has come to last
Forever....
From today
Until tomorrow
As you read this again
Today
And again
Tomorrow
Because it is
Forever.....

It's A Wooden Bridge
That Leads
To Memory Gardens

Let the spirit of a soldier
Cross my bridge
Where the soul of a veteran
Comes to rest
As I remember him
Like yesterday
With honor
And respect
And still today
He comes back
To take watch
Over me
So that I
Can rest in peace
As he watches
Over me
Just like
He has always done
From that of the past...
As we cross over
The wooden bridge
To memory gardens
That will remain
A thing
Of the past

Is it okay

He doesn't know
If its ok
To go outside
And play

He doesn't even know
His name

So he tries
To use other names
Along the way

Just to say
He belongs to someone

And that he is apart
Of something
Along the way

She's my Cinderella
and here I'm
just holding
her right slipper
But if I had my way
I would much rather
be holding her
Instead of her slipper
But there is still time
For my dream
to come true
As we end up
Holding one another
In a fairy tail
That came true
For she
Is my Cinderella
A dream
Come true

Where the green grass grows

It's always greener
On the other side
But if you look close
You will see
That it is only
Color coated
On the other side
Of that barbed-wire
That stands between
You and me
As you travel down
Some ole country road
That's always divided
By the other side
Of the green grass
That seems to grow
In the yard
Of the white picket fence
That only you
Will ever see
From the other side
Of that barbed-wire fence
That still divides
You and me...
As you stand
On the green grass
That grows beneath
Your own feet...
As we look
Over the horizon
Of the barbed-wire
Where the green grass grows...

My bible and my gun

Someone once said
How can you preach
With a bible
In one hand
And a gun
In the other
And I simple said
The constitution
And the bill of rights
Of the united states
Gives me that right
So that I can...
As I stand
To protect her
And this land...
Because faith
Without deeds my brother
Is dead...
For it is written
In the bible as well
In the book of james
So let me tell you this
With freedom of religion
In one hand
And the right
To bear arms
In the other
For they will always
Go together
Hand in hand...
With each other
As I take this stand
With a signal hand
Over my heart
As I speak these words
That you my friend
Will always hear
When I say
I pledge allegiance
To the flag

Of the united states
Of America
And to the republic
For which it stands
One nation
Under god
Indivisible
With liberty
And justice for all
So if this offends you
In any way
Well
That's just too bad
As I believe
In the constitution
Of the united states
That shall read
We the people
Of the united states...
For there is still
So much more
Than what meets the eye
As it is written
From the blood
Of our hands
And translated
To the constitution
That gives us these rights
For there is still
So much more
That you need to read
All because
You do not see...
What has been written...
Beginning
With our freedom
And ending
With the same
So need I say more...
As a soldier
Of the united states
Who will defend

The constitution
That has been written...
So really
Do I need to say more...
Besides these words
Semper fi
And god bless

We are here to stay...
And if you don't like it....
Then get the HELL OUT....
Because this is
The Land Of The Free
And The Home Of The Brave
Where Soldiers Like Me
Will Come To Meet
Because We
Gave Something Of Ourselves
For The Freedom
That You Have
Today
Just Like Those
That Stand Here
Before ME...
And Still
There Will Be More
That Will Come
After Me...
As We Rock This Place
And Let No Others
Tear It Down...

SSGT RALPH LEE BUTLER, JR.

You can take away my pencil
Or even my pen
But you will never
Take away my words
That are written within
And you can go ahead
And break my pencil
Or even my pen
But you will never
Break the words
That I feel
Or even
that I see
Cause they are already written
On a blank piece of paper....
That only I
Can truly see
As I read them
Once again
To you and me...
For they
Are the hidden words
That you can not see
On a blank piece of paper
That only I
Will ever see...

CPSIA information can be obtained
at www.ICGtesting.com
Printed in the USA
FFOW02n1915221014
8255FF